Sex and the Cynics

Sex and the Cynics

Talking About the Search for Love

Edited by Tony Watkins

Copyright © 2005 The Damaris Trust

First published in 2005 by Damaris Books, an imprint of Authentic Media, 9 Holdom Avenue, Bletchley, Milton Keynes, MK1 1QR, UK and 129 Mobilization Drive, Waynesboro, GA 30830-4575, USA

The right of the authors to be identified as the authors of this work has been asserted by them in accordance with the Copyright, Designs and Patents Act 1988.

All rights reserved. No part of this publication may be reproduced or transmitted in any form or by any means, electronic or mechanical, including photocopy, recording or any information storage and retrieval system, without permission in writing from the publisher.

British Library Cataloguing in Publication Data

A catalogue record for this book is available from the British Library

1-904-753-11-6

Unless otherwise indicated, all Scripture quotations are taken from the *Holy Bible*, New Living Translation, copyright © 1996. Used by permission of Tyndale House Publishers, Inc., Wheaton, Illinois 60189, USA. All rights reserved.

Coverdesign by fourninezero design
Typeset by GCS, Leighton Buzzard, Beds,
in 11 on 13 Palatino
Print management by Adare Carwin
Printed in the UK by Haynes, Sparkford, Yeovil, Somerset

Contents

Introduction to the *Talking About* series vii
by Tony Watkins

Acknowledgements xi

Introduction xiii
by Nick Pollard

1. Happily Never After? 1
   by Nick Pollard

2. Up Close and Personal – A Biblical Perspective
   on Love 15
   by Steve Tilley

3. You Complete Me 33
   by Caroline Puntis

4. Desperately Seeking Something 47
   by Annie Porthouse

5.	Love Actually – Study Guide by Steve Couch	63
6.	Closer – Study Guide by Louise Crook	73
7.	Eternal Sunshine of the Spotless Mind – Study Guide by Caroline Puntis	81
8.	The History of Love – Study Guide by Tony Watkins	91
9.	Out of Control – The Philosophy of Arthur Schopenhauer by Peter S. Williams	101
Background to the Quotes		117
For Further Reading		127

Introduction to the *Talking About* Series

Have you ever had one of those conversations when you know you ought to be able to bring in a Christian perspective? The problem is how to do it. As the conversation goes on you become more and more anxious. You know you have a good opportunity to say something; you know you *should* say something – but you just can't think what. Probably all of us have been there at some time or other. Many of us would like a little help on thinking through some issues beforehand.

It seems to me that there are three areas of conversation which frequently cry out for a Christian angle to be included: personal issues in the lives of friends, family or work colleagues; big issues in society generally; and things in the media. They often overlap, of course. So when Nick Pollard was asked to contribute a regular column for *Idea*, the Evangelical Alliance's magazine for members,[1] it seemed a great opportunity to focus on some of the overlapping issues which people are talking about. The articles aim to help readers understand some of what is being said about these issues in today's world, and particularly to explore some of the underlying ideas. The primary aim, of course, is to help equip people for having more and more productive conversations with friends, colleagues and family. It soon became apparent that this is just the kind of help that many Christians feel they need.

So, this series of short books came to be. Each of the books takes the basic ingredients of what Nick has written in one of his articles and develops them into something more substantial, but still light and easily digested. Nick significantly develops his 800-word *Idea* article into the opening chapter of each book. Then come some extra ingredients: a biblical perspective on the issue; articles on key aspects of the central theme; study guides on relevant films, books or television programmes (note: these may contain plot spoilers); and an introduction to one or more key thinkers whose work still influences our culture. Some of these chapters have been developed from material published on Damaris' CultureWatch website (www.culturewatch. org), others have been commissioned especially for this book. Finally, sprinkled throughout the mix are some great quotes which help to spice up your conversations about the issues we're examining (many of these quotes have come from another great Damaris resource, www. ToolsForTalks.com – a collection of tools for speakers whether they are teaching the Bible to Christians or engaged in evangelism. You'll find some background information on these quotes at the back of the book).

This is not the kind of book to sit down and read straight through. Instead it has been designed for dipping into. Each of the chapters stands independently of the others, though of course they're all linked by the common theme. One of the consequences of this is that you will, at times, find a little overlap between chapters. We've minimised this as much as we can without taking away anything essential from one or more of the chapters. The study guides are suitable for individual reflection or for use in home groups. If you do use them in a group setting, don't slavishly work through all the questions – we've given you more than enough so that you can select some that you feel are particularly helpful to your group. Finally, the last chapter, introducing an influential thinker, is inevitably harder going than earlier chapters – which is why it is at the end of the book. It is worth taking time to try to understand the line of argument and why it is significant, but the chapter is not essential for getting to grips with the central issue around which the book revolves.

We hope you will find this interesting, entertaining and stimulating. But our prayer is that this will enable you to be more effective in talking about the good news of Jesus Christ within today's world, whether – as Nick frequently says – you are talking from a pulpit or over the garden fence.

Tony Watkins

Note

[1] For more information, contact Evangelical Alliance at 186 Kennington Park Road, London, SE11 4BT or visit their website: www.eauk.org

Acknowledgements

I am extremely grateful to all the writers who have contributed to this book, and to the series as a whole. It is a joy to work with people who are so committed to thoroughly analysing aspects of our culture in order to help Christians in their discipleship and evangelism, and to help those who are not yet Christians begin to see the extraordinary relevance of the Christian faith.

Particular thanks go to Nick Pollard whose insightful writing is the foundation for the books, and who provides many helpful suggestions on material for inclusion. Thanks also to Steve Couch, Managing Editor of Damaris Books, for his constant support during the many stages of pulling the books together, and to the team at Authentic Media who handle the production of the books, and with whom we enjoy a strong partnership.

Introduction

'I don't believe in it. I wish I could, but I can't.'

The lady who said this to me was not referring to my Christian faith, or even the basic question of God's existence. She was talking about love. For her, love was something she used to believe in as a child, but no longer. She had been hurt too much and now didn't want anything to do with it.

I have met others who have not yet given up on the concept of love. They keep looking for it. But from their experience they know that every time they think they have found it, it never lasts.

Then there are those for whom love is a very real and vital part of their lives. I am immensely grateful that I find myself in that category. As my wife and I approach our 28th wedding anniversary, I can only say that, in my experience, love just gets better and better.

I know that my experience is different from those in the other two categories above. And I know that there are many other categories, and sub-categories in this modern culture.

What is clear is that the word *love* can mean very different things for different people. That causes a problem for us Christians since we want to tell people the wonderful good news that God loves them. This means that we have to use the word *love* – but when we do, we may know what we mean by it, but what do they hear? Do they hear what we mean? This is a problem we face with many words that we want to use when we talk about the gospel. In today's culture they are often heard very differently from how we intend them. Suppose, for example, that we want to tell people that, 'God provides forgiveness for your sin because he loves you.' Quite apart from the overall meaning of the sentence, what do those individual words mean to people in today's culture?

Obviously there are big differences between people. But for many, *God* is a flexible term that covers whatever spiritual concept we want to believe in, *forgiveness* means being excused or 'let off', and *sin* means the mistakes that we couldn't actually help because nothing is really our fault. And that is even before we get to the word *love*. So, in many cases, when we are talking about the Christian gospel, we first have to make sure that people will understand what we mean by the words we use.

For some words this is a fairly simple process. However, this is not the case with the word *love*. This is an intensely personal term which cuts right to the heart of our life experience. It evokes thoughts, feelings and memories that, for one person might be truly wonderful, yet for another could be extremely painful.

That is why, if we are to help people to understand that God loves them, we must take time to understand what different people think of love. That is what this book is designed to help you to do.

Nick Pollard

We are all searching for someone. That special person who will provide us what's missing in our lives. Someone who can offer companionship or assistance or security. And sometimes if we search very hard, we can find someone who provides us with all three. Yes, we are all searching for someone. And if we can't find them, we can only pray they find us.

Mary Alice in *Desperate Housewives*, series 1, episode 11 – 'Move on'

1. Happily Never After?

Nick Pollard

There was once an academic conference that defined love as:

> 'The cognitive-affective state characterized by intrusive and obsessive fantasizing concerning reciprocity of amorant feeling by the object of the amorance.'

That's not the most romantic definition I have heard. Try using that over a candle-lit dinner! I actually prefer the definition offered by a 4-year-old girl who, when asked what love is, thought for a while before replying, 'Love is when two people think that they are pretty – but no one else does.'

Whatever terms one uses to define love, the fact is that, as the introduction to the film *Love Actually* said, love is all around us. We watch films about love, we read books about love, and we listen to songs about love. But, for many people, real love remains at best elusive, and at worst impossible. That may be your experience, or that of your friends. So, let's look at two different (but related) perspectives on love and see how these might affect your friends' understanding of the concept that God loves them.

First, we will look at those who have given up on love altogether. Then we will look at those who are hoping for love but not expecting it to last. In each case we will dig into some philosophical exploration of the subject, both the kind of philosophy that you find in libraries and the kind that you find in cinemas. But our goal will be to think through how we might be better at helping such people to discover that, no matter what their life experience has been, there is a God who loves them and longs for them to come into a relationship with him.

Cynical About Love

Martin Seligman is a psychologist who became famous in the 1970s through his research into the effect of having (or not having) control of our environment. Like many at that time, he carried out his research by doing terrible things to animals. For example, he would put a dog into a box which delivered an electric shock through the floor, but contained a lever that would turn off the electricity if the dog pressed it. Of course, the dog jumped around, frantically searching for a way out, and eventually knocked the lever by accident. After repeating this several times, the dog learned to press that lever as soon as the electricity was turned on. Meanwhile, Seligman put other dogs in a box where there was no way that they could escape the pain. Initially they, also, would jump around, but there was no lever that they could knock into and then learn to press. For them there was no way that they could escape the shock. So eventually they would give up, sit down, whimper, and accept the pain. This was as one might expect. But more surprising was what happened if the second set of dogs was then placed in the first box. They did nothing. They didn't even try to escape the pain. Indeed, even if there was an open door that they could easily walk through to get away from the shock, they did not take it.

Seligman coined a term to describe what had happened to these dogs – he called it 'learned helplessness'. He said that these dogs had learned to be helpless; they had learned that there was nothing they could do to make any difference to the pain they were experiencing, and so they just accepted it.

This concept was then applied to human experience. Very few of us have been placed in a box and subjected to electric shocks. But many of us have experienced other sources of pain – particularly emotional pain. And we, too, can learn helplessness if we have experienced enough times when we have been unable to do anything about it. We won't sit and whimper like Seligman's dogs, but we will develop a pessimistic cynicism that is expressed in phrases such as, 'Why bother?' or, 'What's the point?'

Many of the people who tell me that they do not believe in love describe a process in their lives that has been rather similar to the experience of Seligman's dogs. There was a time when they were positive about love, when they believed that it was real and was really for them. But then they went through experiences that changed all that. Their search for love had produced unavoidable pain and they came to the conclusion that love does not exist – at least for them anyway.

Many such people will identify Mike Nichols' latest film *Closer* (Columbia Pictures, 2004), which tells the story of the interplay between two men and two women over several years. This is surely an ironic title since the four main characters in this film are never close, and never get closer. They have sex with each other, in various combinations, but there is no real intimacy. The sex is used as a weapon. What should be a means of expressing love is used as a tool to manipulate other people. And they also use words in this power-play – words that should draw people close in fact push people away. For example, even when they 'confess the truth' to each other, this is used as a tool to manipulate the other rather than a means of drawing them into a real, intimate relationship. It is significant that this film was directed by Mike Nichols who, almost forty years previously, had directed *The Graduate* (United Artists, 1967) – a film about a young man's relationship with a girl and her mother. Here, as well, sex was used as a power-play and the lover's words were not to be trusted.

There are many today for whom these two films, almost forty years apart, sandwich together their lifetime experience of the pain that love can bring. They reflect their belief that what some call love is actually just a manipulative power-play. Such a cynical view has been explored and expressed not just on the cinema screen, but also by philosophers through the centuries. It goes back a long way to, among others, a group of thinkers in the ancient world called The Cynics or the 'dog philosophers' (from the nickname of Diogenes of Sinope – one of its best known proponents). The Cynics believed that happiness would come from being set free from any emotions or desires that tie people down. For them, love was a bad thing because of all the emotion that comes with it, good and bad.

Another example is the nineteenth century German philosopher Schopenhauer. He thought that the human will was carried along by mindless, aimless, non-rational urges. When he then applied that to a consideration of love, he condemned it as a blind, mindless striving of the will. According to Schopenhauer, love is nothing but the inherent drive to reproduce, that blinds us to reality and ties us to the misery of an unsatisfied hunger. Arguably, Schopenhauer's greatest influence on contemporary culture has not come directly from his writing, but through his influence on novelists and composers, many of whom have expressed his cynicism through their art. Take, for example, Wagner's opera *Tristan and Isolde*. This was written after Wagner had read Schopenhauer's *World As Will and Representation* (apparently reading it four times over!) and had been hugely influenced by it. So Wagner's opera tells the story of a couple's inappropriate, but unavoidable, passion for each other – which tragically destroys them both.

Many today will identify with the outcome of Wagner's opera, with the cynicism of Schopenhauer and with the bleakness of Mike Nichols' *Closer*. And this has a profound effect upon the way in which they hear the gospel message. Suppose we try to tell them the good news, 'God loves you'. How might they react to that? If they really do have the view of love outlined above, we will probably find that they will not want to listen to us – not necessarily because they don't believe in *God*, but because they don't believe in *love*.

If it was the case that they just didn't believe in God they may be quite willing to discuss the point. In my experience, atheists and agnostics are keen to argue about God's existence. However, people who don't believe in love are much less likely to want to talk about it. That is understandable. It is possible to talk about the existence of God in an abstract, academic manner. But one cannot talk about the existence of love in such a dispassionate way. It is a much more personal subject which exposes our sensitivities. Therefore, telling such people that God loves them often results in a dismissal rather than a discussion – they simply don't want to talk about it. They will often assume that the Christian is clearly naive and doesn't understand life – and certainly doesn't understand them.

Before we consider how we might help such people, let's look at another type of person: someone who may also have had bad experiences, but who is trying to hold on to a hope for love. They may believe that love exists, but not that it ever lasts. Such people would not think of themselves as cynical about love in the manner of Schopenhauer, and would probably refer to themselves as 'realistic' about love. They hope for love, they expect love, they will probably enjoy stories about love, but they think that in the real world love always goes wrong.

Real About Love?

This view of love has been illustrated recently in a run of films which each worked from a very similar formula: combining cynicism and fairy tale fantasy.

How To Lose a Guy in 10 Days (Paramount, 2003) tells the story of a male advertising executive and a female magazine writer who are in conflict with each other because he is trying to win a bet that he can make any woman fall in love with him, and she is researching a story on how to make a man want to dump her. In the romantic climax, the conflict is resolved through them falling truly, madly, deeply in love with each other.

Down With Love (Twentieth Century Fox, 2003) tells the story of a female writer and a male journalist who are in conflict with each other because she is trying to show that women do not need romantic love and he wants to prove her wrong. In the romantic climax, the conflict is resolved through them falling truly, madly, deeply in love with each other.

Intolerable Cruelty (United International Pictures, 2003) tells the story of a female gold-digging divorcee and a male divorce lawyer who are in conflict because they are trying to outwit each other by manipulating divorce settlements. In the romantic climax, the conflict is resolved through them falling truly, madly, deeply in love with each other.

These three films are essentially the same story with plot variations. Most of the film is spent showing how 'love' can be deceptive and manipulative. Then, in the last few scenes, the story changes to present a fairy tale ending in which the protagonists fall in love with each other. This makes great cinema. But, does anyone really believe that the characters will now live happily ever after? Or do we suspect that, actually, if the film were to run for another few minutes we would see that the so-called love would fall apart as it always does? And do we find ourselves thinking, 'I like to pretend that there would be a happy-ever-after, but I know there wouldn't be.'

Such a view was recently expressed very clearly and explicitly in the film *Eternal Sunshine of the Spotless Mind* (Momentum Pictures, 2004). In a jumbled mixture of flash-backs, this told the story of Joel (Jim Carrey) and Clementine (Kate Winslet) who had met and begun a relationship on a beach at a friend's barbecue. Both Joel and Clementine are unconventional, but in very different ways. Although they enjoy their life together, inevitably their personality differences mean that they clash and argue. One day, after a furious row, they separate. But then Joel decides that he wants to try to work things out, and so he goes to visit her at her workplace. He cannot believe her reaction – she doesn't even recognise him. Joel discovers that she has undergone a revolutionary new treatment that has completely wiped him out of her memory. Incensed by this, Joel undergoes the same treatment.

The story so far will be familiar to many who have fallen in love and then experienced conflict and pain in the relationship. It is what happens next in the film that explores so well the real dilemma that many such people face. Joel and Clementine meet again, and begin to fall in love once more. But then they come across the audio tapes that they made before they had their memories erased. They hear what happened, how they got on each other's nerves, how they became angry with each other, how they separated.[1] Now, the question arises, if they know that this will happen, will they put themselves through it all again? Is the shared joy of the relationship worth the inevitable pain that they know they will experience?

This is a dilemma faced by many people. The fact is that, in many people's experience, love is a powerful emotion that evokes great pleasure but also leads to great pain. This was expressed recently in the popular television series *Desperate Housewives*. This tells the story of a group of women who live in Wisteria Lane, in American suburbia. Our narrator is Mary Alice (Brenda Strong), who at the beginning of the first episode talks us through her own suicide. She introduces us to all the mourners at her funeral, and her female friends. The women are all housewives, and they are all desperate in their different ways. At the end of episode 14 ('Love is in the Air') she says, 'It's impossible to grasp just how powerful love is. It can sustain us through trying times, or motivate us to make extraordinary sacrifices.

It can force decent men to commit the darkest deeds, or compel ordinary women to search for hidden truths. And long after we're gone, love remains – burned into our memories. We all search for love but some of us, after we've found it, wish we hadn't.'

One of the reasons why *Desperate Housewives* has been such a success is that it seems to resonate with so many people (not just housewives) who view love in this way. Suppose we try to tell them the good news, 'God loves you'. How might they react to that? If they really do have the view of love I have just outlined, we will probably find that they may listen to us. But will they really hear what we are saying?

If they are willing to believe that there might be some kind of God (however they might understand him to be), they might be willing to believe that this God could love them. But what will they think that this love will mean? Probably not the eternally satisfying, fully committed, self-giving love that we see described in the Bible and demonstrated in Jesus – because they don't believe that this kind of love exists.

Therefore, it is important that we help them to understand what love can be, what it can mean. In the same way, looking back to the other group of people (who are cynical about love), we must help them to understand that love can actually exist at all.

Biblical About Love

Whoever we are talking to, we will always want to lead them into the Bible where they will discover what God says about love. En route to that, we might find it helpful to look at elements of a biblical perspective on love which have been illustrated in recent films.

Let's look at two examples: *Meet the Fockers* and *Love Actually*.

Meet the Fockers (United International Pictures, 2005) is the sequel to *Meet the Parents* (United International Pictures, 2004). Greg and Pam, planning to get married, bring their parents together for a few days. There follows a huge culture clash as the relaxed, liberal, laissez-faire lifestyle of Greg's parents meets the uptight right-wing interventionist approach of Pam's.

Amongst all the humour, one thing that the film illustrates is the importance of life-long commitment. Indeed, the plot only works because these two couples are still together after all their years of marriage. There are tensions within the couples (which are echoed in the tensions *between* the couples), but they are committed to staying together for life. Whether we identify with Greg's parents or Pam's, we see an illustration of real love lasting through a lifetime commitment to each other.

Love Actually (Universal International Pictures, 2003), has been described as a celebration of love. It demonstrates the power of the love between man and woman, parent and child, brother and sister, and even just good friends. It demonstrates how love crosses the barriers of age, culture, language and social divide. And yet this film is set in gritty reality; it is not a fairy story. The characters sweat and swear, they laugh and cry, they experience temptation and suffer from unfaithfulness.

One thing that *Love Actually* illustrates is the importance of self-sacrifice. This is illustrated in many ways. We see an author (played by Colin Firth) learning a new language in order to communicate with the girl he met while abroad. We see a prime minister (played by Hugh Grant) going door to door in a dodgy part of

London to find his girl. We see a successful rock star (played by Bill Nighy) giving up a celebrity party in order to be with his old and rather boring friend. We see an office worker (played by Laura Linney) give up the chance of a night of passion to be with her psychotic and desperately vulnerable brother. We see an artist (played by Andrew Lincoln) keep himself away from the woman he believes is perfectly beautiful, because she is married to his best friend. And so the stories of sacrificial love go on.

So, some recent films give us the opportunity to talk about the importance of commitment and sacrifice. Perhaps that then provides a way of taking us into talking about the Bible's message, particularly summed up by Paul as:

> 'Live a life filled with love for others, following the example of Christ, who loved you and gave himself as a sacrifice to take away your sins.' (Ephesians 5:2)

Note

[1] For a fuller summary of the plot of this film, see chapter 7, p. 81

People ... seem to know everything about sex but very little about love.

Rowan Pelling

2. Up Close and Personal – A Biblical Perspective on Love

Steve Tilley

> 'Ours is a culture crying out for intimacy, but only able to conceive of accessing it through sex.'[1]

Gabriel Jacoby has a problem. Actually, in David Baddiel's novel *Time for Bed*, he has lots but we will dwell only on one. 'She wants me to talk to her during sex. I don't know what to say.'[2]

Gabriel, like many other characters in books and movies, can only conceive of accessing intimacy through sex, but when asked to behave intimately during sex struggles to know what else is required. Sex and intimacy have been confused. They've become separated and put back together incorrectly. But no one told us it was meant to be this way. So we forget that sex belongs best in the context of an intimate relationship and that an intimate relationship is possible without sex. The Bible says that the truth about sex and intimacy has always been plain for us to see. How did we miss it?

God has shown us everything we need to know about him and his world and the way it is meant to work (Romans 1:19), but we have managed to exchange the truth of God for a lie and this upset has also spoiled our understanding of sexuality (Romans 1:25–26).

Intimacy and the Old Testament

There are two parallel creation narratives at the beginning of our Bibles – Genesis 1:1–2:4 and Genesis 2:5–25. According to the first account, in the beginning, intimacy between Creator and created is stressed. God created human beings for intimate relationship, with himself and with each other. There is intimacy of relationship in the Godhead, expressed by the plurals: 'Let us make people in our image, to be like ourselves' (Genesis 1:26) and 'God patterned them after himself' (Genesis 1:27). And having done this, he commanded the greatest act of intimacy from them: 'Have a lot of children!' (Genesis 1:28, CEV).

In the second account, the intimacy of relationship between the man and the woman is explained by a story of the woman's unique creation, from the rib of the man. In this version it causes the man to exclaim, 'She is part of my own flesh and bone!' (Genesis 2:23). The narrator goes on to say, 'This explains why a man leaves his father and mother and is joined to his wife, and the two are united into one' (Genesis 2:24). The narrator saw intimacy all around and found the inspired explanation that this very intimacy must come from God. It must arise out of the way people have been made.

But that intimacy is lost. Genesis 3 is the account of the loss of relationship with God. After disobeying God's only rule, Adam and Eve do not talk intimately with God but hide (Genesis 3:8). The loss of intimacy escalates. The first man and woman are thrown out of the Garden of Eden and here begins the Bible's account of a human quest for a return to intimacy with our creator, with the substantial disadvantage of original and continuous sin. But it is possible still to find some intimacy of relationship. People find ways to worship God (Genesis 4:26). We are reminded that God created men and women to be like himself (Genesis 5:1).

Angry that God is not pleased with his offering (we are not told why), Cain kills his brother Abel (Genesis 4:8). Despite the displeasure God is said to feel about the relationship with his creation (Genesis 6:6), a man, Noah, is found who pleases God (Genesis 7:1). After saving Noah and his family from the flood, Noah's sacrifice is a pleasing aroma to God (Genesis 8:21). Yet soon after the waters subside, something strange has gone on between Noah and his sons following a bout of drunkenness, which once again jeopardises intimacy (Genesis 9:20–27).

We have dwelt at length on the early chapters of the Bible for good reason, but the rest of our scriptures deal with the wavering relationship between God and his people, sometimes pleasing him, often displeasing him.

Saul's son Jonathan loved David, Saul's successor as king, as much as he loved himself. He swore a binding covenant to keep their families friends for all time (1 Samuel 18:1; 20:13b–17). On more than one occasion they promised absolute loyalty to each other (1 Samuel 23:18). But this loyalty came at a price, Jonathan more than once having to choose between his friend and his father – a father whom God had ceased to help (1 Samuel 18:12). David's lament after Saul and Jonathan's death in battle is truly moving:

> 'How beloved and gracious were Saul and Jonathan!
> They were together in life and in death.
> They were swifter than eagles; they were stronger than lions.
> O women of Israel, weep for Saul,

> for he dressed you in fine clothing and gold ornaments.
> How the mighty heroes have fallen in battle!
> Jonathan lies dead upon the hills.
> How I weep for you, my brother Jonathan!
> Oh, how much I loved you! And your love for me was deep,
> deeper than the love of women!
> How the mighty heroes have fallen!
> Stripped of their weapons, they lie dead.'
> (2 Samuel 1:23–27)

Again and again we learn, as the Queen comforted the American people after 9/11, that grief is the price we pay for love.

In the Song of Songs we have nothing less than a collection of erotic, poetic literature, perhaps designed to have been read as part of a marriage celebration. In a world today where the image rules, it is a triumph to read some words – and in the Bible no less – which put sexual desire, in the context of committed love, on a pedestal. Whilst something may have been lost across the stretches of time, culture and translation with, 'Your teeth are as white as sheep, newly shorn and washed' (Song of Songs 4:2), there is no doubt that these are the words of a couple who want each other physically. Several hundred years later the lyrics of many contemporary songs regularly confuse love (a desire for companionship or comradeship with commitment) with lust (a desire for a physical relationship). Something has gone missing.

The scriptures refer again and again to wonderful, fulfilling, inter-human relationships which have moments of great – and costly – intimacy. Sadly, there are many more examples, too numerous to mention more than a few, of relationships falling apart.

The great leaders of the Old Testament were all flawed. David, the great king, committed adultery. Moses, the great leader, murdered an Egyptian; he was punished for his people's continuous moaning against God. Solomon, the wisest of all kings and leaders, was pointed in the direction of other gods by his many wives and concubines. Even in those books which perhaps owe as much to literature as to history, we find intimacy compromised. Jonah runs from a God of compassion because he prefers to hate and condemn. Job questions God to seek reasons for his suffering whilst shaking off the advice of his friends and so-called comforters.

The Old Testament is the account of the desire to restore intimacy. God longs that his people would be obedient to him and we see the consequences of them not doing so. The books of the Law more than hint at the need for the blood of a sacrifice to pay the penalty for disobedience. The prophets, particularly Isaiah in the central chapters 40–53, show us that the substitution of an appropriate servant will be required to atone for the sin which has spoiled relationships. Again and again it is found impossible for created and Creator to have a restored relationship in terms of mere human effort, driving the apostle Paul eventually to say, 'I don't understand myself at all, for I really want to do what is right, but I don't do it. Instead, I do the very thing I hate' (Romans 7:15). Although written in the New Testament this is a fantastic summary of where the Old Testament leaves us. The need for atonement is a subject we will consider in the next section.

The theme song of the great pop festivals of the 1970s was Joni Mitchell's 'Woodstock' (1970, performed by Matthew's Southern Comfort), which talked about the need to get back to the garden. Getting back to the garden is the human quest, but it is impossible. Occasional moments of intimacy can be manufactured, but we must never confuse half a million people enjoying Bob Dylan with a true recovery of relationship. Those festivals were allegedly the place of free love but may simply have been places of free sex.

Today we find our levels of intimacy wavering. On occasions we enjoy the strength of relationship with one another which comes through complete commitment. On others, we step back from the sacrifice required truly to put another person's interests ahead of our own. Our popular culture mirrors this back to us, showing us characters in search of intimacy yet often pulling back. Our Bibles show us that the instinctive feeling we have, that intimacy is to be pursued, is God-given. It also acknowledges that our efforts will fall short.

In one of the greatest, but perhaps less well known, pieces of Old Testament literature, the small book of the prophet Hosea tells of God's call to him to marry a prostitute. This marriage, says the Lord to Hosea, represents my love for my people. You are going to carry on loving your wife despite her unfaithfulness, just as I carry on loving my creation despite its failure to reciprocate. You are even going to give your children from this marriage ritual names: Jezreel meaning *God scatters*, Lo-ruhamah meaning *No mercy* and Lo-ammi meaning *Not my people* (Hosea 1:2–9).

Intimacy is always on God's agenda. From searching in the garden (Genesis 3:9) to allowing the great prophet Isaiah to approach despite his unclean lips (Isaiah 6:6–7), the initiative is always God's. He makes the first move. After Hosea's wife had abandoned him, God told him to go after her all over again, mirroring God's intention to undo those ritual names and gather, show mercy to, and reinstate his people. His final move, anticipated by Isaiah, the work of seeking and saving the lost, is achieved once and for all in Jesus. Which takes us into the New Testament and the territory of Luke 15.

Intimacy and the New Testament

In Luke 15 we learn that lost things matter to God. God gets as excited about the return of a sinner as a woman finding a missing coin, a shepherd forgetting his safe sheep in order to parade the missing one, and a father welcoming back a son who had wished him dead (which is effectively what asking for the inheritance 'now' amounted to).

We must remember that these images would have been shocking to Jesus' audience. Offensive even. In those days women were not trusted to give evidence in court, shepherds were despised (which is partly why Jesus called himself the 'good shepherd') and Jewish fathers were expected to be disciplinarian not liberal. Jesus turned his hearers' world upside down by suggesting God might be something like a woman, a shepherd and what they would think of as a bad dad. Whatever you are like, you will be excited at finding something that you thought lost. God shares that excitement with everyone. Whatever our occupation or personality, we should be enthusiastic at relating to those currently lost to God

The Christian Gospel is that Jesus Christ is the one true sacrifice (Hebrews 9:26), the substitute (1 Peter 2:24) and servant (Acts 8:32–35) whose death paid the price of human sinfulness, satisfying God's justice and continuing, in practice, to demonstrate his love for his creation.

From the earliest of days, the Christian understanding was that Jesus Christ was, and remains, the Son of God (Matthew 16:16). Consequently the search for a reinvigoration of that intimacy which God intended ends in Christ. In him the price has been paid for the rebellion that lost us intimacy and we can, with boldness, call God *Abba*, Father, and be treated as his own children (Romans 8:15–16).

Jesus is the great repairer of the greatest possible relationship – the relationship between humans and God, created and Creator. His life and death show us the way of sacrificial love – he laid down his life for his friends. That reconciliation makes possible a more powerful reconciliation with others than we could ever achieve on our own terms. For from *agapē* (Christian love) springs *koinonia* (fellowship). Church fellowships and communities will often feel a bit like porcupines huddling together for warmth on a cold night (more warmth = more hurts). But when two people relate to each other by both relating to God, there is the possibility of a new depth of relationship between them. Outsiders will not understand, but will be amazed if and when they find it for themselves.

Our human relationships will always fall short of Jesus' life-giving example, although we will come across amazing stories of self-sacrifice in a world where people are made in the image of God. It is simply that in a fallen world we will encounter far more stories of spoiled relationships, lost intimacy and unrequited love.

Commitment to relationships is on the decline. In a throw-away society with fast-everything and 'Buy now, leave us the money in your will!' offers not quite available but seeming like they are, it is hardly surprising that people feel comfortable disposing of a relationship and picking up another at the first sign of difficulty. But sex. Well that's another matter. Love may be all around but sex is everywhere. 'The inheritance of [Generation] Xers[3] is to live lives emotionally numbed but sexually aroused.'[4]

The Bible and Sex

God gets very poor publicity on the subject of sex. To hear people talk you would think he was against the idea. But Christians believe he invented it. Loneliness was the first thing God declared not good (Genesis 2:18), and being fruitful and multiplying (Genesis 1:28) was his first instruction. However, all the rest of the Bible's words on sex – all of them – are attached to a negative instruction. Clearly sex is a dangerous commodity, easy to misuse and misunderstand.

Populating the earth is no longer the principal motivation governing most people's sex lives. Birth control methods have allowed the separation of breeding and pleasure. We are in charge of our sex lives in a way that the first humans could not possibly have imagined. This means that we can have a physical relationship without emotional commitment.

But Genesis 2:24 tells us that a sexual relationship belongs in the context of long-term commitment – leaving home and living with a partner. 'Sex outside a context of trust and permanence . . . is the art of telling lies. It is saying physically what I could never say in words: "I commit myself to you absolutely, permanently, vulnerably".'[5]

The rest of the Bible's teaching on sex condemns sexual immorality without indicating beyond all doubt what that might involve. It must have been more apparent to its early readers/hearers. The list of those who 'will not inherit the kingdom of God' (1 Corinthians 6:9) includes:

pornoi	fornicators or 'those who indulge in sexual sin'
moikoi	adulterers
malakoi	male prostitutes
arsenokoitai	homosexuals

No one has been able to put the argument convincingly that the Bible condones sexual activity outside the husband/wife relationship. Those who affirm same sex relationships point to the Bible's cultural limitation rather than any positive teaching accepting them. The current, mainstream Christian view is that sexual intercourse belongs in a lifelong marriage relationship between two people of opposite gender. A powerful dissenting minority, however, want to say that the Bible's prohibitions about same-sex relationships are culturally bound. They insist that permanent, same-sex relationships are not sinful and should also be valued. As many of you know, this argument threatens to split the church.

The Bible and Love

Hebrew

The Hebrew word *ahab* means *to love, to like* or *to be a friend*. It is sometimes used of romantic love. *Ahaba* is more intimate. It includes family love and is often used of romantic love. It is also used in some passages to show the intensity of God's love. Neither *ahab* nor *ahaba* mean a physical act of sexual love.

The perfectly ordinary word *yada* translated as *to know, recognise* or *understand* is also used to mean an intimate sexual relationship. The Authorised Version of the Bible translates *yada* as 'Adam knew his wife' but our modern translations either say 'lay with', 'slept with' (New Living Translation) or ignore it completely and say that Adam and Eve had a son (Genesis 4:1).

Greek

It is often reported that the Greeks had several words which we translate with our word *love*. They made a clear distinction between erotic and non-erotic love:

> 'The Greeks ... spoke of *agapē*, altruistic love (in Latin *caritas*, which gives us – but with what a cold ring – our word 'charity'). They spoke of *ludus*, the playful affection of children and of casual lovers, and *pragma*, the understanding that exists between a long-established married couple. They spoke of *storge*, the love that grows between siblings or comrades-in-arms who have been through much together, and of *mania*, which is obsession. And they allied the latter with *eros* or sexual passion.'[6]

In Jesus' encouragement to his disciples to obey his commands and thus show their love for him, the word used is *agapē*, which is primarily used in the New Testament to mean Christian love but occasionally means simply concern or interest. In the great hymn to love in 1 Corinthians 13 the word being discussed is *agapē*. It is also *agapē* which is being encouraged when the letter to the Ephesians tells husbands to 'love your wives with the same love Christ showed the church' (Ephesians 5:25). The first aspect of the fruit of the spirit is *agapē* (Galatians 5:22).

'... the Greek word for love in the New Testament, *agapē*, was not previously in common use. It was taken into the Greek of the New Testament specifically because the love of God, seen in Jesus of Nazareth, required a new word. God's love completely transcends all human ideas or expressions of love.'[7]

However, Don Carson has argued that there is much overlap in meaning between *agapao* (the verb form of *agapē*) and *phileo*[8] (which usually means love but can also mean *like* and occasionally *kiss*). He says one cannot read too much into the choice of word, particularly in passages such as John 21 where Peter is reinstated, Jesus asking him if he loves him using both words. This seems to be de-emphasising the special nature of the word *agapē*, but there can be no doubt that *agapē* is the word most often chosen by the New Testament writers to denote Christian love, or the distraction of loving other things.

English

Despite the great richness of the English language we face a certain poverty when it comes to the word *love*. What we mean by it is dependant on context:

'Certainly, when we consider the love of chocolate, of freedom, God's love for the world, romantic passion and maternal care, it seems plausible to suppose that the word "love" has a different import when it is used to refer to these different things. The love of chocolate does not seem to share a subtle essence with maternal love and neither of these seems to be the same as romantic love. When it comes to chocolate, "love" functions as an extreme version of "like".'[9]

Mike Starkey wrote:

> 'Most of my contemporaries no longer make love. They shag, bonk and screw – quickly, anonymously, lovelessly. The generation more pitifully searching for intimacy than any other in history has taken the central sacrament of interpersonal intimacy and killed it dead. We have the dubious privilege of living in the culture which is presiding over the death of eroticism.'[10]

Biblical Love in Action

The life of a Christian is therefore two-faced, by which we mean looking in two directions. It is about constantly seeking that intimacy with God which Jesus has made possible. But it is also about looking out for the needs of others, for by so doing we show love in action.

It has often been said that this is a love which turns the world's values on their head. This is a love which foregoes any possibility of revenge (Matthew 5:39), prays for people who ill-treat you (Matthew 5:44), and, avoiding any hint of prejudice, treats others the way you would like to be treated yourself (Luke 10:36–37). And, indeed, takes up its own cross (Matthew 16:24).

This is love as response, loving God because he first loved us. Not to earn salvation, for that has been achieved already, but to demonstrate gratitude. The Victorian hymn writer George Matheson puts it like this:

> 'O Love that wilt not let me go,
> I rest my weary soul in Thee
> I give Thee back the life I owe,
> That in Thine ocean depths its flow
> May richer, fuller be.'[11]

If this had ever been easy, straightforward and achievable, the New Testament would probably have ended after the book of Acts. But the letters to the early church from Paul, Peter and John needed to be written to correct behaviour in churches where there were squabbles, disputes and arguments. Even saved people row from time to time. The relatively well-known passage in Ephesians setting out rules for the new life in Christ suggest to us that the early church in Ephesus was a place of lies, anger, theft, dirty talk, bitterness, curses and rudeness (Ephesians 4:25–32). Why prohibit them if they weren't happening? Maybe my church isn't so bad after all.

This is the life that we noticed in chapter one, observing not the early church but the movies. People do fall in love but it doesn't last; things that start as endearing do become annoying. Affection does turn to argument – and people often split up. Relationships are ditched rather than rebuilt. It does all seem so inevitable.

But biblical love in action is an intention not a result. It is about a willingness to come back and try again having erred. It is about forgiving one another and being forgiven. Again and again.

It is biblical love which is expressed in the marriage service where partners agree to take each other:

> '. . . for better, for worse,
> for richer, for poorer,
> in sickness and in health,
> to love and to cherish
> till death us do part . . .'[12]

This is an unconditional promise. Whatever the other partner does to you, your promise stands. It is a covenant, not an agreement. It is a high standard not completely reproduced in a civil ceremony where there is some choice over the words to be used.[13]

The letter to the Ephesians has the highest possible standard for a husband, that he should love his wife as Christ loved the church and be prepared to give his life for her (Ephesians 5:25). A marriage lived like this is a picture of Christ's love for his church.

Conclusion

We fool ourselves if we think sex is intimacy. All over the world people are enduring, rather than enjoying, loveless sex, routine sex and dull sex, searching for the hit of an orgasm as a momentary high. We throw ourselves into it as part of our search for intimacy, but it is at worst shallow, if not completely false.

We also fool ourselves if we think that both partners being Christians is the secret to long-lasting marriages. Such naïvety is often brought up short by a nasty dose of realism. 'All have sinned; all fall short of God's glorious standard' (Romans 3:23). Christians too. It won't be easy.

But intimacy is not impossible. It hasn't been tried and found wanting. It has found itself set aside by a popular culture which increasingly sees relationships as a disposable commodity. The Bible offers hope that genuine love is accessible and possible but does require effort, sacrifice and determination.

Above all it requires an admission that if I am human, so are you. If I can sin then so might you. If I live my life with an expectation that any relationship slightly spoiled can be dropped at once, I am going to have emotional learning difficulties. It is in the melting pot of human sinfulness, disappointing behaviour and second chances – a million second chances – that true intimacy is learned.

And then you learn to say that your friends are your friends and nothing they can do could possibly jeopardise that relationship. You will visit them in prison if necessary. Even if the friend is your spouse. You'll be there for them.

Notes

[1] Mike Starkey, *God, Sex and Generation X* (Triangle, 1997)
[2] David Baddiel, *Time For Bed* (Warner Books, 1996)
[3] Generation X is often defined as those born between the early 1960s and the mid 1980s.
[4] Mike Starkey, *God, Sex and Generation X*
[5] Mike Starkey, *God, Sex and Generation X*
[6] A. C. Grayling, *The Meaning of Things – applying philosophy to life* (Phoenix, 2002)
[7] David Prior, *The Message of 1 Corinthians* (*The Bible Speaks Today* series) (IVP, 1985)
[8] D. A. Carson, *Exegetical Fallacies* (Baker Book House, 1994)
[9] John Armstrong, *Conditions of Love – the philosophy of intimacy* (Allen Lane, The Penguin Press, 2002)
[10] Mike Starkey, *God, Sex and Generation X*
[11] George Matheson, 'O Love that wilt not let me go', *Mission Praise* (Combined) no. 515
[12] Church of England marriage service, *Common Worship* (Church House Publishing, 2000)
[13] The choice of words must, however, be approved by the Superintendent Registrar.

There's two things I learned in life, kid: you find someone to love and live everyday as if it were your last.

Joe in the film *Alfie*

3. You Complete Me

Caroline Puntis

Everyone loves a great story. Not everyone, however, would pay money to go and see a 'love story' at the cinema, whether it's a manufactured 'rom com' or a period drama tragedy. Certainly not every movie that claims to be about love tells a great story – the kind that stays with you long after the lights come up and you return to real life.

Whether it all ends in heartache or happily-ever-afters, from time to time a moment of truth lights up our screens, leaving us reaching for the tissues, a notebook or even a Bible. Sometimes the vulnerability of a character speaks volumes:

> 'I'm just a girl, standing in front of a boy, asking him to love her.' (*Notting Hill*, 1999) [1]

At other times, the sheer frankness makes us wonder if love is really worth the risk:

> 'Now that I've met you, would you object to never seeing me again?' (*Magnolia*, 1999)[2]

Here's a selection of such scenes from some of the films that have stayed with me.

'We live in a cynical world . . . I love you. You complete me.' (Jerry, *Jerry Maguire*, 1996)[3]

These days when it comes to relationships, love seems to be quite a long way down the agenda. Jerry Maguire, played by Tom Cruise in Cameron Crowe's movie of the same name, is introduced as a successful and honest, but misguided, businessman. As a sports agent to the stars, he is loaded with status and wealth. He and his fiancée Avery have a relationship that seems to be just about great sex and climbing up the social ladder. Jerry's track record with women is set out in his bachelor party tribute: good at friendship, bad at intimacy, cannot be alone. We get the impression that life satisfaction isn't something he experiences at a deep level – Jerry has been seduced by his own image of success.

When Jerry gets fired, he invites other employees of the business to leave with him and start a new business. Only one person has the courage to join him – the hapless Dorothy Boyd (Renée Zellweger), a single mother whose life runs at the other end of the social spectrum to Jerry's.

It is not long before Maguire loses his only big client, which doesn't go down too well with his fiancée:

> 'I don't tell a man who just screwed up both our lives, "Oh, poor baby. That's me, for better or worse ... But I do love you"!'

Suddenly, the truth that we've known since the start of the film hits Jerry like a ton of bricks. He replies,

'There's something missing here, don't you think?' Love is the one thing that this relationship is not about.

Crowe's film does not take the easy way out. Some time later, Dorothy and Jerry get married, but their relationship is not loving – Jerry still can't do intimacy. He sees love in others – in the joyful marriage of his one remaining client; in a deaf man who signs, 'You complete me' to his girlfriend – but doesn't experience it himself. Eventually Dorothy brings the relationship to an end, telling Jerry that she thought her love would be enough for both of them – but it wasn't. She reflects,

> 'On the surface, everything seems fine. I've got this great guy. And he loves my kid. And he sure does like me a lot. And I can't live like that. It's not the way I'm built.'

Dorothy was there for Jerry when everything went wrong; when success finally comes and the client wins big, he is alone. But the feeling he experiences is no longer simply the need to be with anyone, it is specific – he loves Dorothy. He races home to tell her the good news.

Cameron Crowe takes another character on a similar journey to find out what love is really about in his film *Vanilla Sky* (2001).[4] David Aames, also played by Tom Cruise, once again has wealth and status, a 'friend', Julie Gianni (Cameron Diaz), to have occasional sex with – but no love. Early on in the film, David falls in love with a beautiful woman called Sofia (Penélope Cruz). Julie, however, is in love with David and resents him for using her for sex. She follows him to Sofia's apartment and offers to give him a ride when he comes out in the early hours of the morning. On the way, her resentment comes out and she asks him:

> 'Don't you know that when you sleep with someone, your body makes a promise whether you do or not?'

She then drives them off a bridge, killing herself and leaving David with a face that cannot be put back together again. He tries to pick up with Sofia where they left off, but the reality is that they were only acquaintances who had a few hours of fun together. The story is told through David's dream that they lived happily ever after. When this dream turns into a nightmare, the truth is revealed and a choice lies before him: to try living the dream again, or to take a risky exit back into reality. David chooses real life, with all its possibilities. As he prepares to face a new kind of future, he is reminded of Sofia's words to him:

> 'Every passing minute is a chance to turn it all around.'

Crowe's preoccupation seems to be with taking his characters to a place where they are forced to realise what love is and how much it costs.[5] The things that had appeared to add up to the value of love – success, wealth, status, sex, beauty – actually add up to nothing and cannot give the characters' lives any meaning. When these things are lost, love gets a look-in and becomes central to the characters' existence.

'Two things I learned in life, son: find someone to love and live every day as though it were your last.' (Joe, *Alfie*, 2004)

Alfie (Jude Law) is the archetypal playboy: scooting around New York city; rarely sleeping in his own bed; tasting the delights of various women who adore his

English charm. The fact that he leaves behind a trail of broken hearts fails to make any kind of dent in his conscience. Why should it, since he always tells his lovers up front that he will never commit?

It is only when a health scare forces him to take some time out from his busy seduction schedule that Alfie turns his thoughts to the question of, 'What's it all about?' At the hospital, he meets an old-timer called Joe (Dick Latessa), who suggests that life is all about being with someone you love and making the most of every moment. But Alfie gets the all clear and sees no reason to stop using his job as a limo driver to pick up glamorous, rich women.

Then Nikki (Sienna Miller) appears, and Alfie wonders whether she could be the woman to hold his attention. He breaks his long-standing rule to never invite women back to his apartment. But her stay turns out to be more than he bargained for. After a perfect beginning, this 'high calibre' woman who looks so great on the outside reveals how broken she is on the inside. As Alfie considers her true nature, he pauses to reflect on a school trip that introduced him to the beauty of the female form – a marble statue of a Greek goddess. His initial awe soon turned to disappointment when he realised that the marble was covered in cracks, chips and imperfections. The statue was ruined. He tells the viewer:

> 'That's Nikki, a beautiful sculpture – damaged, in a way you don't notice 'til you get too close.'

When the consequences of his philandering finally catch up with him, Alfie breaks down in self-pitying tears: he has a child – with his best friend's girlfriend. He turns to Joe for advice, who tells him:

> 'Alright, you screwed up . . . The question is, what's going to happen with the rest of your life?'

Alfie resolves to let his guard down and tell his favourite lover, Liz (Susan Sarandon), how he feels about her. At last, the turning point we've been waiting for arrives – Alfie gets a taste of his own medicine. Liz reveals that she is with a younger man . . . younger than Alfie. Suddenly, he is in the place of countless women he has tossed aside. As he applies his own exacting standards to himself, the truth dawns:

> 'Despite my best efforts I'm beginning to feel some small cracks in my faux finish . . . My life's my own, but I don't have peace of mind. And if you don't have that, you've got nothing.'

The message is clear: love isn't about finding a perfect person; it happens in spite of the imperfections.

'I'm going to talk to you about whether or not you want to get married – to me.' (Rob, *High Fidelity*, 2000)[6]

Rob Gordon's[7] (John Cusack) somewhat unromantic proposal is a major turning point in his life. As with other characters from Nick Hornby's novels also made into films – Paul (Colin Firth) in *Fever Pitch* (1997),[8] Will (Hugh Grant) in *About a Boy* (2002),[9] Ben (Jimmy Fallon) in *Fever Pitch* (2005)[10] – Rob is unwilling to commit. There is always a 'what if' associated with thoughts of settling down, along with an untiring self-absorption that leaves each character at arm's length from the women in their lives. *High Fidelity* begins as Rob's girlfriend Laura (Iben Hjejle) moves out. He reflects:

'I can see now I never really committed to Laura. I always had one foot out the door, and that prevented me from doing a lot of things, like thinking about my future and ... I guess it made more sense to commit to nothing, keep my options open. And that's suicide. By tiny, tiny increments.'

Rob has to work out that the realities of this relationship are as good as it gets, and that he needs to give up on the idea that someone better might come along. In spite of himself, he has reached a point in his life where

'I'm just sick of thinking about it all the time ... love and settling down and marriage, you know. I want to think about something else ... Other women ... they're just fantasies, you know, and they always seem really great because there's never any problems ... And then I come home and you and I have real problems ... I'm tired of the fantasy because it doesn't really exist ... It never really delivers ... And I'm tired of everything else for that matter. But I don't ever seem to get tired of you, so ...'

Having explored the difficulties of making a commitment, Hornby turns his attention to a marriage some years down the line in his novel *How to be Good*.[11] Katie's analysis of her marriage in crisis inevitably draws her to consider what love means in the long term. She discovers 1 Corinthians 13 through Lauryn Hill's sung rendition[12] and comes to the conclusion that love is not about winning battles with your husband. She decides to stay with him, having worked out that this is the right thing to do, but knows it will not be easy. There are no romantic celebrations – whether anyone will dare to make a faithful film adaptation of this story, with its evidently less than happy ending, remains to be seen.

'Please let me keep this memory. Just this one.' (Joel, *Eternal Sunshine of the Spotless Mind*, 2004)[13]

For all the beginnings of love that bring in the crowds with their happy endings, many stories explore one attribute that characterises love in the real world – trying again. As Rob discovers in *High Fidelity* when Laura returns, love 'keeps no record of when it has been wronged'.[14]

An extraordinary film that explores the possibility of an absolute fresh start is *Eternal Sunshine of the Spotless Mind*, a second collaboration between screenwriter Charlie Kaufman and director Michel Gondry.[15] Joel (Jim Carrey) and Clementine (Kate Winslet) are hardly what you would call a well-matched couple, rather they seem to be a case of 'opposites attract'. After one particularly bad falling out, impetuous Clem goes to a doctor who practises a procedure that erases unwanted memories. Clem 'erases' Joel from her mind and continues her life without him. When Joel finds out, he decides to do the same. Kaufman's screenplay takes us into Joel's mind for the duration of the erasure process as he goes back in time to the first memory of Clem. As he gets through the painful recent past and encounters the happy memories from earlier on in their relationship, Joel realises that he does, in fact, love Clementine. With despair, Joel cries out in his mind to the doctor to stop the procedure, but it's too late.

As the final memory of their first meeting on a beach in Montauk fades away, the Clementine of Joel's mind whispers, 'Meet me in Montauk.' When Joel awakes the next day, oblivious to the procedure that has erased his memory during the night, he feels compelled to go to Montauk. Once again he sees Clem on the beach, and the attraction begins again. They should have been none the wiser, but one of the doctor's disgruntled employees sends out tape recordings to each client with their reasons for going through the erasure process. Clem unwittingly puts her tape into Joel's cassette player as they drive along and inexplicably hears herself saying the worst imaginable things about Joel. He throws her out of the car, only to find a similar tape waiting for him when he gets home. As he listens to his ranting about Clem, she appears with an apology. It seems that their new relationship cannot possibly withstand the revelations that expose both of them, and what were apparently their real feelings for one another. Clem starts to leave, but Joel stops her.

> **Joel:** I can't see anything that I don't like about you.
>
> **Clementine:** But you will ... you will think of things. And I'll get bored with you and feel trapped because that's what happens with me.
>
> **Joel:** [casually] Okay.
>
> **Clementine:** [laughing] Okay!

The film closes with Joel and Clem laughing as they chase each other along the beach at Montauk. The essence of their decision, their longing to have another go because somehow they know, deep down, that it will be worth it, reminds me of God's word to his people through the prophet Hosea:

> 'And now, here's what I'm going to do: I'm going to start all over again. I'm taking her back out into the wilderness where we had our first date, and I'll court her. I'll give her bouquets of roses. I'll turn Heartbreak Valley into Acres of Hope. She'll respond like she did as a young girl, those days when she was fresh out of Egypt.'[16]

Perhaps the reality that the characters in these films find is that it is tempting to start all over again with someone new, but in the end, it's not as good as starting again with someone you love. This truth is surely part of the story we find ourselves in. Every time we try to live without him, God shows us love by repeatedly inviting us back for more – in anticipation of the ultimate 'happy ever after'.

Notes

[1] Directed by Roger Michell, screenplay by Richard Curtis; released on DVD by Universal Pictures Video (1999)
[2] Written and directed by Paul Thomas Anderson; DVD released on DVD by Entertainment in Video (2000)
[3] Written and directed by Cameron Crowe; released on DVD by Columbia Tri-Star Home Video (1997)
[4] Written and directed by Cameron Crowe – a remake of *Abre Los Ojos* (dir. Alejandro Amenábar, 1997) written by Alejandro Amenábar and Mateo Gil; released on DVD by Paramount Home Entertainment (2002)
[5] Advance details of Cameron Crowe's forthcoming (at the time of writing) film *Elizabethtown* suggest that it, too, is exploring this issue.
[6] Directed by Stephen Frears, screenplay by D. V. DeVincentis, Steve Pink, John Cusack and Scott Rosenberg; released on DVD by Buena Vista Home Entertainment (2001)
[7] In Nick Hornby's novel on which the film is based, Rob's surname is Fleming.
[8] Directed by David Evans, screenplay by Nick Hornby; released on DVD by Cinema Club (2001)
[9] Directed by Chris Weitz and Paul Weitz, screenplay by Peter Hedges, Chris Weitz and Paul Weitz; released on DVD by Universal Pictures Video (2002)
[10] Directed by Bobby Farrelly and Peter Farrelly, screenplay by Lowell Ganz and Babaloo Mandel

[11] Viking, 2001/Penguin, 2002
[12] 'Tell Him' from *The Miseducation of Lauryn Hill* (Columbia, 1994)
[13] Directed by Michael Gondry, screenplay by Charlie Kaufman; released on DVD by Momentum Pictures Home Entertainment (2004)
[14] 1 Corinthians 13:5
[15] Their first project was *Human Nature*, 2001
[16] Hosea 2:14–15, *The Message*, translated by Eugene H. Peterson (NavPress, 2004)

It changes your life when you enter into a marriage and it can change it just as much when you're part of a break-up.

Jude Law

4. Desperately Seeking Something

Annie Porthouse

You know when a TV show has made it: the characters come to life – people forget they are nothing more than the creation of the writer! So if you stick *Desperate Housewives* into Google, and follow up the links, you'll soon find the question posed: *Which one are you?* Answering a few simple questions will reveal to you what you've always longed to know – which resident of Wisteria Lane you most resemble. Whether you suspect you're a 'simple Susan', a 'glamorous Gabrielle', a 'bragging Bree' or a 'labouring Lynette' – or none of the above, it is very clear that *Desperate Housewives* is a huge hit.

A saucy blend of melodrama, whodunit, dark comedy with plenty of all-round 'weird' factor, it is strongly comparable to *Twin Peaks*, a quirky series from the early nineties. *Desperate Housewives* presents the lives of four seemingly perfect women, residing in a picture-perfect, upper middle-class American suburb – a fresh and contemporary take on 'happily ever after'. The beautiful women have beautiful homes, with accompanying manicured lawns and manicured nails; but there's trouble brewing in the pleasantly scented air. The pilot episode presents us with ordinary housewife

Mary Alice committing suicide for no apparent reason. It is she who enlightens us about the residents of Wisteria Lane, from her unique and somewhat elevated vantage point. Now it is not just the appearance of her small circle of friends that she can observe, but each and every slice of reality – however zany, however messy, however dark.

The four central characters are Susan, Lynette, Gabrielle and Bree. Susan is a dippy divorcee and book illustrator who lives with her bright and feisty teenage daughter. It isn't long before Susan's eyes turn towards new neighbour Mike, the hunky plumber. Lynette is the former businesswoman who has traded the boardroom for boredom, raising four disruptive children under the age of six, while getting minimal assistance from her busy-at-work husband. This woman is stressed. Gabrielle is a former model whose husband Carlos wants the world to know how wealthy he is. But why does she turn to her teenage-stud gardener for sex? Will Carlos find out, and what will the consequences be if he does? Finally, Bree is a domestic diva who doesn't like to fail – ever. When it comes to running her household, appearance is everything. What will be her prim and proper response to situations that threaten her image – and to what lengths will she go to keep up the illusion? Whatever their situation, one thing is evident: they are all desperate. Perhaps for sex, money, status and power – but more likely for love, fulfilment and contentment; for others to accept and appreciate who they really are.

Wisteria Lane: the road to success

In terms of what makes a television success story, *Desperate Housewives* has broken all the rules. Instead of starting out as a reasonably popular show that gradually picks up steam and pulls in its audience by word of mouth, it has become an instant and major hit, both in the States where it was born and now over here in the UK. Millions of viewers have found a trip along Wisteria Lane the perfect antidote to yet more crime investigation spin-offs and dodgy reality-TV clones. This is highly clichéd, and has been said about every good novel and film under the sun, but it is what social critics are still saying when it comes to *Desperate Housewives*: we love it because we can relate to it. We can identify with the characters – women with needs, desperate needs – who have real-life issues to face, but don't always have the resources or the ability with which to tackle them. Nearly all TV housewife-types are presented to us as having flaws, from Marge Simpson through to Pauline Fowler. But when it comes to love, sex and relationships, this new breed of housewives really knows how to screw up! They strike a chord with us because, although we might hate to admit it, we can see ourselves in them. So we empathize with *Desperate Housewives'* efforts to deconstruct the American Dream. The houses may look perfect inside and out, but in reality there is a marked disparity between this superficial perfection and the characters' inner desperation and frustration; their longing to love and be loved. *Desperate Housewives* has many similarities with films such as *American Beauty*, which was also centred on such deconstruction.

We might relate more to desperation for money and power (Gabrielle) than for domestic perfection (Bree), or for the kids to start behaving (Lynette) or for a man who can deal with our lack of culinary expertise (Susan), but essentially the one thing we all connect with is the desire to be truly loved. Not just a fling, but loved; not just dating, but loved; not even just married and settled, but loved; loved by our neighbours, our friends, our children, our parents, our partners and our spouses. We crave a love that accepts us as we are, with all our quirky defects and acquired life baggage.

Real Women

'But surely this isn't new in terms of TV?' some of you will be asking. When Carrie finally opted for Mr Big over the sculptor Aleksander Petrovsky in sexy Paris, fans were not happy – not because of her decision (any *Sex in the City* addict will tell you it was clearly the right one) but because it meant it was all over. The final conclusion to a plot line which had run for six years marked the end of the show – and the end of an era. If *Friends* saw some of us through our late teens and early twenties, it was *Sex in the City* that saw us through the next phase. But then ... nothing. It was as if all 'quality escapism' American comedy shows had packed up and left the airwaves for good. I turned thirty on the first of January 2005, with the knowledge that I was forever doomed to watch *Friends* and *Sex in the City* re-runs; to de-program what I already knew of the plots in the hope that they would ever remain fresh and sassy. Until, that is, I discovered *Desperate Housewives*.

But does *Desperate Housewives* really differ much from those earlier favourite shows? Compare the characters in *Desperate Housewives* with those in *Sex in the City*:

- Susan/Carrie – single and a bit dippy.
- Bree/Charlotte – traditional and obsessed with perfection.

- Lynette/Miranda – career women with a dry sense of humour.
- Gabrielle/Samantha – sexually voracious, attracted to glamour.

The difference is that *Desperate Housewives* is about women who have grown up and done a great deal of what they set out to do. The searching is over; they don't need to find their place in the world any more. So our singleton is now a divorcee, the career woman has had to give it all up to care for her kids, the perfectionist has a real family to deal with (one with imperfections galore), and the glamorous one has managed to marry money but is now both bored and dissatisfied. So while Carrie and friends could waffle on about sex and men, and men and sex, all day (with small breaks for actual sex and for expensive lattes) the desperate housewives aren't afforded such luxury. Being a bonafide housewife doesn't hold as much pizzazz as living it up in the city. There are nappies, toddler tantrums, awkward teenagers, trying boyfriends and husbands, and the like. The new foursome on the block live with the choices and relationships they have settled on – or at least, they give it their best shot.

Sex in the Suburbs?

And so to love. Is there any genuine love to be found anywhere, or is this really 'Sex in the Suburbs', as many have claimed it to be?

When it comes to being cynical about love, glamour-girl Gabrielle springs to mind – she seems to have given up on real love. If her marriage with Carlos appears not to involve any authentic love, then her secret relationship with John the gardener has even less. Carlos seems to value her as his wife, but very much puts himself and his work/wealth first. Gabrielle is not totally naive – she resents this but has learnt to live with it. After all, the marriage suits her too – she doesn't actually have to do anything with her day other than shopping for over-priced, yet highly desirable designer clothes and shoes. Conversely, John seems to offer her love but Gabrielle brushes it aside. For her, sex with John is all about just that and no more – on tap, instant, gratifying with no strings attached. It boosts her self-esteem without her having to give anything back by way of commitment. Gabrielle knows that she has the upper hand: John won't let on to Carlos about the affair. He wouldn't dare – or at least he didn't until the very last episode of the first series. So sex is a weapon for Gabrielle, and a very effective one too. If she wants something from Carlos she can use her body to get it. When Carlos and his mother think that paying $15,000 a year for a maid is a bit extravagant, Gabrielle happens to mention during sex with him that if she had to do all the housework she would be too exhausted to give him this kind of service on a regular basis. Carlos agrees and the maid stays.[1] She can also use withdrawal from bedroom activity as the ultimate weapon – as when Carlos insists she sign a post-nuptial agreement and she refuses to let him share their bed until he's dropped the idea.[2] Marriage, for Carlos and Gabrielle, seems to be primarily about status, convenience and regular (or not so regular) sex, with perhaps a little companionship thrown in for good measure.

But Gabrielle is not the only cynic. There's another neighbour, Edie, who has an annoying habit of bedding anything in trousers that takes her fancy. Sex is something of a hobby for her which doesn't need to be bothered by love:

Edie: That's my new contractor. We're sort of dating.

Lynette: Didn't you once say you never mix business with pleasure?

Edie: No, I said never mix pleasure with commitment.

Lynette: [laughing] Right.[3]

I think it is safe to say that the majority of the *Desperate Housewives* characters are pessimistic about love, although they are not quite as cynical as Gabrielle and Edie. Their expectation of some form of legitimate loving relationship only goes as far as to expect very little; the bare minimum – something that will be for a while, but might be whisked away when they least expect it. 'Happily ever after' is only for fairy stories and Hollywood, not for here and now.

Take Lynette. What she desperately craves (as well as a good night's sleep) is for her and husband Tom to have a loving relationship in the same vein as when they first got married before the offspring made an appearance. She cannot abide his long hours away from the family and she feels isolated. As her friend from beyond the grave reminds us: 'Humans were designed for many things – loneliness is not one of them.'[4] Lynette's pessimism seems to be linked to her view of what love can be, and also to the circumstances she finds herself in. She finds herself up against everything: difficult kids, exhausting days, seeing so little of Tom, sometimes a lack of sex in their relationship,[5] him working alongside his ex-girlfriend,[6] and so on. Lynette's lack of faith in Tom's loyalty eventually leads her to sabotage his big promotion; her jealousy wins over any genuine love she has for him as well as her ability to see what's best for him.[7]

Susan could possibly claim the title of 'exception to the rule'. She is one of the few who is actually quite positive about love. But her optimism seems to be based on her naivety. She is prepared to move in with Mike purely on the basis of her feeling for him, regardless of her friends' continuing doubts about his suspicious activities. Even having been badly hurt by her husband in the past (who left for his secretary), Susan goes on believing that things could work out for her again.

Then we have those characters who claim to be in love, but who are in fact gripped by obsession. There's George, Bree's creepy psychotic pharmacist, who develops an unhealthy interest in far more than her pharmaceutical needs. He's so unhinged that he even tampers with her husband's medication in an attempt to kill him. There is little love involved when trying to destroy someone's marriage or attempting to eliminate their husband. At best this approach to love is highly distorted. And take John, Gabrielle's gardener. John naively assumes she would leave the wealthy and well-connected Carlos for him, a teenage, penniless lawn-cutter, despite her protests that she's only after his toned and tanned body:

Gabrielle: I'm unhappy with Carlos and my marriage. I feel like I don't have options, and it's driving me crazy. Every time something went south in my life, I always had a plan B. Now I feel like I have nothing.

John: What about me? Can't I be your plan B?

Gabrielle: Damn it, John. What is our new rule?

John: Stop pretending we have a future.

Gabrielle: Thank you.[8]

John thinks he's in love with Gabrielle, but really his predicament is being 'in lust' with her, and being young and naïve (as opposed to scheming and dangerous like George). But it still highlights an unfortunate and misplaced view of love.

So if the cynic and pessimist's perspective on love is insufficient, and if sex, lust, naïvety, infatuation and obsession aren't the stuff of love, then what is? 1 John 3:16–18 indicates that if you see someone in need but don't attempt to meet that need, then you are devoid of love for them. This happens continually in *Desperate Housewives* – people looking after themselves first, and addressing the needs of others as and when it fits into their schedule. The same can be said of many of us Christians – we are not always that good at putting others first. The way of the world is to shower ourselves with so much love that we have little left over to spread around to our family, friends and those in need. Harsh words? Possibly. Perhaps this only applies to me (though at least I'm honest!).

C. S. Lewis has a theory that the human loves can, in fact, become gods in our lives. Sex is an obvious example, and possibly its positive spin-offs such as having our self-image affirmed. Even our friendship or affection for others can become distorted. Once we put ourselves at the centre of the picture and push the recipient of our love to the margins, we know that the 'love' is largely based on self-interest. For example, Bree assumes she loves her children when she tries to control them. Essentially though, she shows very little interest in finding out what they actually want in life; her main concern is herself. What will *her* family look like if son

Andrew comes out as being gay?[9] What will *she* look like if the children leave her and the family home to live with their father when she and Rex divorce?[10] No doubt she does have some heartfelt love for them, but it appears to have taken second place to her own desires and wishes. Of such love Lewis suggests, 'they become our gods: then they become our demons. Then they will destroy us ... [they] can become in fact complicated forms of hatred.'[11]

What does 1 John tell us is our only example of true love? That Jesus died for us. We may never be able to give out such amazing love; many say that no love is one hundred percent altruistic. But God's love was and still is. Once we know his love we can begin to share it with others. So does this mean that, since *Desperate Housewives* doesn't include any wholeheartedly positive Christian characters, there is no true love? Not for a minute! All of us are made in the image of our creator, even the likes of Susan, Bree, Lynette and Gabrielle. So glimpses of genuine love are bound to be seen in us now and then. As Lewis says, 'The human loves *can* be glorious images of Divine love.'[12] So we see Lynette accompanying her difficult elderly neighbour to hospital:

Mrs McCluskey: Lynette, where are they taking me?

Lynette: You're going to the hospital, Mrs. McCluskey. You're gonna be fine.

Mrs McCluskey: I don't want to go alone. Come with me.

Lynette: Oh, um, these are trained technicians, and I've got a roast in the ... freezer.

Mrs McCluskey: Please. I'm scared.

Lynette: Yeah, I'll come with you ... Okay, here I am.

Mrs McCluskey: Thank you.[13]

Later Lynette agrees to visit Mrs McCluskey on a regular basis to ensure she takes her medication properly, and also that she has at least some form of human companionship – the thing she so clearly longs for. There's nothing in it for Lynette. She's busy; she's not related to Mrs McCluskey and will get no payment for her time. No, she shows a lonely woman some genuine love, knowing that loneliness makes for a miserable life.

We also see Susan letting her mother Sophie stay with her when Sophie splits up with her fourth husband. It doesn't suit Susan one bit and Sophie regularly drives her nearly insane. But she battles on and shows her mother genuine love, despite the annoyance and embarrassment she brings. This sort of self-sacrificing love, seen in real life or in a script that is modelled on real(ish) life, is a reflection of God's love. In fact, it demonstrates to the world – though the world rarely realises it – that God's love is real, not some abstract idea thought up by hymn-chanting Bible-bashers of old. Without God's love at work in the world, we could never know such genuine love, flawed though our version of it is.

Let's hear it for love then: unconditional, self-giving love found in places where you would not really expect to find it. This kind of love is found not so much between the sheets on *Desperate Housewives*, but more smuggled in between the main plots of each episode – in small doses so brief you might easily miss them. But it's there nonetheless: love that involves both commitment and sacrifice, putting someone else first, putting our own to-do lists aside.

We were all created for a purpose – ultimately to have a relationship with God. But, more generally, it is to have relationships with others: friendships which involve commitment, self-sacrifice, honesty and generosity; friendships between husband and wife, boyfriend and girlfriend, parent and child, neighbour and neighbour. These relationships are not of an identical nature, but they all have the same tune being played in the background – love. Perhaps this explains our obsession with shows such as *Desperate Housewives* (and its predecessors) – we like to watch the friendships. It makes us consider our own set of friendships, and our own role as a friend in life – a giver and recipient of love.

Cynical Suburban Sluts?

I propose that we're all far too cynical on this planet. Firstly, the residents of Wisteria Lane are far too cynical about love – its reality, its potential, its capacity to be unconditional and unending. Their lack of optimism is apparent from minute to minute, scene to scene, plot to plot. They cannot comprehend that their yearning for true friendship and love is actually the result of them being designed to live in relationship with God, and that they will never be truly fulfilled until they know him. However, as viewers of the show we are also far too cynical. Take L. Brent Bozell III, the founder of America's Parents' Television Council. He says that *Desperate Housewives*, 'really should have an even more obvious title, like *Cynical Suburban Sluts.*' Infuriated as he is by what he perceives to be the lack of moral standards in the programme, he urges his supporters to boycott the advertisers (who enable the show to be made). Bozell proclaims:

> 'The advertisers are happy ... and so what if the culture rots. This show's writers might think they're not moralisers, but they are. The moral of this story is: Life's too short and love's too fake to behave with honour.'[14]

Whether we're just a little concerned about the image of love on *Desperate Housewives*, or incensed like Bozell, we are all guilty of pointing the finger. But none of us are experts on the topic or the practice of love – we must leave that to God. Yes, *Desperate Housewives* shows the reality of how love-less life without God can be. But despite the confusion over what love really is – sex replacing love, lust replacing love, obsession replacing love, and so on – in *Desperate Housewives* we can still find some glimpses into the love God created us to give and receive. Not perfect, but conceivably far more real than much of the self-absorbed, sex-related so-called love that we see on our screens day in, day out.

Perhaps without realising it, Marc Cherry, Executive Producer and creator of *Desperate Housewives*, has written something that aptly reflects the situation of humankind, especially humankind living without knowing God's love. If the often-distorted view of love we see in *Desperate Housewives* pains us, then let's use it as fuel to motivate us to become more of a loving person – let the world know that there is a better way. But let's also refrain from casting the first stone. Instead, let's celebrate the love that we *can* see, and acknowledge the desperation to love and be loved. If we think that when it comes to loving relationships, we're above the likes of Susan, Gabrielle, Lynette, Bree and their neighbours, maybe we just need to look a little closer, be a bit more desperate to see God in all of his vast and wonderful creation, not merely in those who have chosen to follow him.

Notes

[1] Episode 6, 'Running To Stand Still'
[2] Episode 19, 'Live Alone and Like It'
[3] Episode 17, 'There Won't Be Trumpets'
[4] Episode 19, 'Live Alone and Like It'
[5] Episode 21, 'Sunday in the Park with George'
[6] Episode 20, 'Fear No More'
[7] Episode 23, 'One Wonderful Day'
[8] Episode 19, 'Live Alone and Like It'
[9] Episode 18, 'Children Will Listen'
[10] Episode 7, 'Anything You Can Do'
[11] C. S. Lewis, *The Four Loves*, p. 13
[12] C. S. Lewis, *The Four Loves*, p. 14, my emphasis
[13] Episode 19, 'Live Alone and Like It'
[14] L. Brent Bozell, 'Boycotts and Catty Girls', 22 October 2004 – www.parentstv.org/PTC/publications/lbbcolumns/2004/1022.asp

[Love] is a word. What matters is the connection the word implies.

Rama Kandra in the film *Matrix Revolutions*

5. *Love Actually* – Study Guide

Steve Couch

Film Title: *Love Actually*
Tagline: It's all about love, actually
Written and Directed by: Richard Curtis
Starring: Hugh Grant, Liam Neeson, Emma Thompson, Colin Firth, Alan Rickman, Martine McCutcheon, Laura Linney, Andrew Lincoln, Keira Knightley, Gregor Fisher, Martin Freeman, Kris Marshall, Billy Bob Thornton
Distributor: Universal
Theatrical Release Date: 21 November 2003
DVD Release Date: 19 March 2004
Certificate: 15

Key Themes

Love, sacrifice, sex, friendship, death, betrayal, communication, family, intimacy, hope, commitment

Summary

Several stories interweave to make the point that wherever you look in life, love isn't far from the surface.

The new Prime Minister (Hugh Grant) falls for his tea-lady (Martine McCutcheon), while his sister Karen (Emma Thompson) faces up to the realisation that her husband Harry's (Alan Rickman) eye has fallen on a young work colleague. One of Harry's other employees, the lonely Sarah (Laura Linney) has to choose between a hot date or caring for her mentally ill brother. Ageing rock star Billy Mack (Bill Nighy) has a surprise Christmas number one, and realises that his friendship with his fat, Glaswegian manager Joe (Gregor Fisher) is the most significant relationship in his life. Writer Jamie (Colin Firth) discovers that his girlfriend and his brother are having an affair, then finds that love can cross language barriers. Mark (Andrew Lincoln) has to reconcile his love for his best friend Peter (Chiwetel Ejiofor) and his infatuation with Peter's new wife Juliet (Keira Knightly). Daniel (Liam Neeson) faces his grief after the death of his wife, while trying to help stepson Sam (Thomas Sangster) to deal with his first schoolboy romance. Colin (Kris Marshall) gives up on finding love in England, and buys a plane ticket to America, confident that his English accent will unlock the hearts and beds of beautiful American girls. John (Martin Freeman) and Judy (Joanna Page) meet while simulating sex acts for a film, yet share a sweet and tentative courtship.

The sheer number of storylines means that many strands are given only the briefest opportunity for character development or story arc. It could be argued that *Love Actually* might have worked better as four or five separate films, allowing the secondary tales a little more room to breathe and a greater share of the spotlight. But that overlooks the intentions of the film. Richard Curtis seems less interested in telling individual stories than in telling the story of love itself: a diverse, irrepressible, all-pervading and essential presence in human life.

Background

Richard Curtis is arguably Britain's most successful comedy screenwriter. On television he has written successful sitcoms such as *Blackadder*, *The Vicar of Dibley* and *Mr Bean*. As a writer for film, he has been responsible for the phenomenal success of *Four Weddings and a Funeral*, as well as other romantic comedies such as *Notting Hill* and *Bridget Jones's Diary*. *Love Actually* is the first time that he has combined his writing duties with those of director.

Born in New Zealand, it is ironic that Curtis has become synonymous with a distinctively British take on the genre of romantic comedy. He was, however, educated in the British public school system – he was head boy at Harrow. A few key ingredients seem to recur in most of Curtis' films. Well-known American leading ladies (Andie McDowell in *Four Weddings and a Funeral*; Julia Roberts in *Notting Hill*; Renee Zellweger in *Bridget Jones's Diary*) add a splash of glamour and transatlantic box-office appeal. Leading men represent various British stereotypes for the international audience (Hugh Grant's bumbling charm in *Four Weddings and a Funeral* and *Notting Hill*, Colin Firth's icy aloofness in *Bridget Jones's Diary*). The supporting cast draws heavily on a repertory company of reliable but lower-profile Brits. The films are not coy about sex, but neither are sex scenes steamily erotic. Swearing crops up regularly, in robustly earthy fashion and always for maximum comic effect.

The recurring feature of his cinematic output, over and above all of these, is that he writes good-hearted films. A Curtis film always tries to leave the audience with a warm glow as they make their way out of the cinema and back into their own lives. We are reassured that love can happen; love can work its magic for us too, if only we are prepared to keep going in the face of whatever apparently insurmountable odds we find ourselves confronted by. Although some of his films are criticised by some for the sexual content and swearing, and by others for the saccharine resolutions of romantic strife, Curtis has done more than anyone else to define the mass-appeal British romantic comedy of the last ten years. His is a formula which consistently delivers box office takings for the producers, and favourites for the DVD collections of couples everywhere.

Curtis' place in Britain's comedy establishment is also anchored by his central role in organising the charity Comic Relief, with its bi-annual invasion of the BBC television schedules to raise both money and awareness for good causes in Britain and in the developing world. He has also taken a high profile role in the campaign Make Poverty History, and included the campaign's awareness-raising white wristband in the 2005 New Year special of *The Vicar of Dibley*. Curtis explains:

> 'Geraldine would have been 20 at the time of Live Aid – and so it seemed a very apt idea for an episode of *Vicar of Dibley* to centre around her trying to mark the anniversary of a day which changed her world. I believe she'd still be totally up in arms about the horrific statistics twenty years on – one child dying every three seconds, unnecessarily, of the results of extreme poverty. Dying of diarrhoea, dying of TB, dying of hunger. Dying simply because they're born poor ... So, I believe, and I'm sure Geraldine would believe, that it's time for us to

say enough is enough. That's why this campaign, Make Poverty History, the White Band campaign, has started. And this year there's a chance we can crack this thing which has been a source of shame for so long.'[1]

Curtis talks and writes eloquently about the injustices in the world. Whether the subject is the foolishness of war, the iniquities of world poverty or the universal human need to be loved, it's clear that Curtis is committed to much more than simply writing funny films and TV shows.

Questions for Discussion

1. The film asserts that 'love actually is all around'. How far do you agree with that statement?

2. 'Whenever I get gloomy about the state of the world, I think about the arrivals gate at Heathrow Airport. General opinion has started to make out that we live in a world of hatred and greed, but I don't see that. It seems to me that love is everywhere.'
   What is the optimism of *Love Actually* founded on? Is this foundation sufficient to justify that optimism?

3. Which of the storylines did you find most involving? Why?

4. Were there any storylines that left you unmoved? Why do you think this was the case?

5. Would the film help somebody to define what love actually is? How would you define love?

6. What different types of love are presented in the film? Which others are missing?

7. 'But God showed his great love for us by sending Christ to die for us while we were still sinners' (Romans 5:8).

    What, if anything, does the film have to say about God's love? Are there any appropriate parallels to be drawn from the incidents in the film to love on the scale described in Romans 5?

8. How would you relate the following Bible passages to the portrayal of love in the film? Romans 13:8–10; 1 Corinthians 13:1–13; Colossians 3:12–14; 1 John 4:7–12.

9. Mark: 'You tell the truth at Christmas.' Natalie: 'If you can't say it at Christmas when can you?'

    What has Christmas got to do with telling the truth?

10. What does the film have to say about intimacy? What was the nature of intimacy for John and Judy, the couple who met while shooting sex scenes for films?

11. What is the effect of infidelity in the film? Which characters are faced with their partner cheating on them, and how do they respond to the discovery of this? Why do you think Karen and Jamie react in different ways?

12. Karen: 'Would you stay, knowing life would always be a little bit worse, or would you cut and run?'

    What advice would you give to Karen? Is forgiveness possible in a situation like this?

13. Why does the Prime Minister have Natalie transferred to a different department? Does he have any right to feel hurt when he sees her with the American President (Billy Bob Thornton)?

14. How did you react to Mark's doorstep profession of love to Juliet? Was it appropriate for him to express his feelings for his best friend's new wife like that? If not, what else could/should he have done? How do you think his friend would react if he found out about the incident?

15. What does the film suggest about the relationship between love and sacrifice?

16. Sam: 'Worse than the total agony of being in love?'
    In what way can love be agonising?

17. The film features three desperate missions of love – the Prime Minister's search for Natalie; Jamie's pursuit of Aurelia (Lucia Moniz) in Portugal; and Sam's evasion of security guards to say goodbye to Joanna (Olivia Olsen). How far would you go to tell someone that you loved them?

Note

[1] www.makepovertyhistory.org/vicarofdibley.html

That's the problem with the institution of marriage – it's based on compromise.

Miles Massey in the film *Intolerable Cruelty*

6. *Closer* – Study Guide

Louise Crook

Film Title: *Closer*
Tagline: If you believe in love at first sight, you never stop looking
Director: Mike Nichols
Screenplay: Patrick Marber
Starring: Julia Roberts, Jude Law, Clive Owen, Natalie Portman
Theatrical Release Date: 14 January 2005
Distributor: Sony Pictures Entertainment
DVD Release Date: 6 June 2005
DVD Distributor: Sony Pictures Home Entertainment
Certificate: 15

Key Themes

Love, sex, relationships, commitment, truth, dishonesty, forgiveness, loneliness, cruelty, hatred

Summary

Closer centres on four people who are looking for love. Dan (Jude Law) is an obituary writer for a London newspaper who believes in love at first sight. The opening scene shows Dan spotting Alice (Natalie Portman) in a London crowd, and the pair stare at each other flirtatiously. In her distraction, Alice – an American stripper – walks out into the road without looking and is hit by a car. Dan rushes to her rescue and takes her to hospital, and their relationship develops from there.

Closer only shows the audience the beginning and end of its characters' relationships (director Mike Nichols says, 'in love, we remember beginnings and endings and tend to edit out the middles'[1]), and so the next scene occurs some months later. Dan has written a novel based on Alice's life, and he has gone to Anna (Julia Roberts) to have a photograph taken for the dust jacket. Dan is now living with Alice, but is instantly attracted to Anna. Dan begs her to meet up with him, but she knows he has a girlfriend and refuses to do so. The film then jumps to the next scene, where we are introduced to the fourth and final character, Larry (Clive Owen). Dan is messing around on an Internet sex message board, and logs on pretending to be Anna. He gets chatting to Larry, a hospital doctor, and tells him that 'Anna' will meet him in the aquarium the next day. The real Anna is, of course, oblivious to this meeting, but, as Dan knows, will be there at the time Larry has been told. In the aquarium, Larry chats to Anna, and although she is utterly confused about how he knows her, she is taken with Larry and they start going out.

The rest of the film charts the relationships between Dan and Alice, and Larry and Anna over four years and the infidelity between the couples that rocks these relationships. The characters' pursuit of sexual pleasure results in power struggles, selfishness and ultimately the emotional destruction of each one of them.

Background

Closer began its life as a play, written by Patrick Marber back in 1997. The stage version has already toured the globe in different forms, including performances on Broadway and in the West End. It won the Laurence Olivier Theatre Award for Best New Play of 1997. Marber was delighted when director Mike Nichols (whose previous films include *Who's Afraid of Virginia Woolf?*, *The Graduate* and *Primary Colors*) approached him about a film version. The play has, of course, been significantly adapted (by Marber himself) for the big screen, but it still feels very theatrical to watch. He says, 'Mike knew the material was so personal, if not autobiographical, that it would have been illogical for someone else to write the screenplay.'[2]

The film relies heavily on its four actors to make it work, and therefore the casting of top quality actors and actresses for the four main roles was essential. Clive Owen was nominated for an Oscar (Best Supporting Actor) and Natalie Portman was nominated for Best Supporting Actress. Both were nominated for a host of other awards such as Golden Globes and BAFTAs. Clive Owen was familiar with the play already having played Jude Law's character Dan in the original London stage production. He says, 'It was like starting all over again because when you play a part you see the whole thing through that character's perspective. Now I had to re-evaluate everything that I thought when I originally did it, switch everything around and see it from Larry's point of view.'[3]

Patrick Marber has described his play as a 'love story' saying, 'It's about other things of course – sexual jealousy, the male gaze, the lies we tell ourselves and those we are most intimate with, the ways in which people find themselves through using others. But in the end, it's a nice simple love story. And as with most love stories, things go wrong ...'[4] Both play and, to a lesser extent, the film contain a lot of anger and the language is very strong. Marber says that *Closer*

> 'provokes a very personal response, and the response to both the play and the film are wildly divergent. People either seem to love it or hate it, and I think a lot depends on how your love life is going at the time! I mean, I'm happily married now, and I wasn't when I wrote it, and that's probably significant. I don't think I could write it like that now, I'd write something different.'[5]

He had to resist the temptation to modify it in the light of his more recent experiences because he felt it was important to be faithful to who he was when he wrote it.

Questions for Discussion

1. What did you think of *Closer?* What kind of emotions did you experience as you watched the film?
2. What would you identify as the main themes of the film?
3. What do you think of the film title *Closer?* To what extent are the central characters closer to each other at the end of the film?
4. How does each of the characters change as the film progresses? What causes each of them to change? What has each character learnt by the end of the film?

Closer – *Study Guide* 77

5. How do the characters exercise power over each other and manipulate each other? Why do they do this?

6. How do these characters view sex? What roles do sexual tension and sexual rivalry play in the film? What is the result of Dan and Anna's infidelity? What light does Proverbs 6:20–35 shed on their situations? What would they have avoided by heeding its advice?

7. How do Dan, Larry, Alice and Anna appear on the outside? How is this different to how they feel inside? Why is there such a difference?

8. Why does Alice hide her identity from Dan and everyone else? What do you think she is hiding?

9. Dan says, 'What's so great about the truth anyway? Try lying for a change – it's the currency of the world.'

    What role does truth play in the film? How does this impact the characters' lives? According to Ephesians 4:17–5:2, what role should truth play in our relationships? What else does Paul say is important for relationships to work? Why do we find this so hard?

10. To what extent do you think that *Closer* reflects the pattern of modern relationships, as many reviewers have suggested? How does that make you feel?

11. Alice asks Dan, 'Where is this "love"? I can't see it, I can't touch it. I can't feel it. I can hear it. I can hear some words, but I can't do anything with your easy words.' Why is Alice so let down by Dan's love?

12. What kind of love are these characters searching for? Why does love disappoint them? See 1 John 4:7–21. What are the implications for us of the fact that God is love and loves us perfectly? How should this reality transform the way you think about yourself and others, and the way you behave?

13. What does this film have to say about human nature? How consistent is it with the Christian view that human rebellion against God is what leads to our self-absorption and to us harming each other (see Genesis 3:1–19; James 4:1–12)?

14. Why are the characters unable to forgive each other? Do they show any awareness of needing forgiveness themselves? Why/why not? How does David respond after committing adultery with Bathsheba (Psalm 51, see also 2 Samuel 11–12)? Why is forgiving others so vital (see Matthew 18:21–35; Colossians 3:12–14)?

Notes

[1] uk.movies.yahoo.com/reviews/2004/Closer.html
[2] Patrick Marber interviewed by Adrian Hennigan – www.bbc.co.uk/films/2004/12/23/patrick_marber_closer_interview.shtml
[3] Rebecca Murray, 'Clive Owen Talks About *Closer*'
[4] Rebecca Murray, 'Clive Owen Talks About *Closer*'
[5] Patrick Marber interviewed by Adrian Hennigan

You think you've found the right man,
but there's so much wrong with him.
And then he finds there's so much
wrong with you. And then it just
all falls apart.

Bridget in the film *Bridget Jones:
The Edge of Reason*

7. *Eternal Sunshine of the Spotless Mind* – Study Guide

Caroline Puntis

Film Title: *Eternal Sunshine of the Spotless Mind*
Taglines: Would you erase me?
I'm fine without you.
This Spring, clear your mind.
You can erase someone from your mind. Getting them out of your heart is another story.
A comedy for anyone with a past they'd rather forget.
Director: Michel Gondry
Screenplay: Charlie Kaufman, Michel Gondry and Pierre Bismuth
Starring: Jim Carrey, Kate Winslet, Kirsten Dunst, Tom Wilkinson, Elijah Wood, Mark Ruffalo
Distributor: Momentum Pictures
Theatrical Release Date: 30 April 2004
DVD Release Date: 4 October 2004
Certificate: 15

Key Themes

Relationships, love, intimacy, memories, forgiveness, forgetting

Summary

Joel (Jim Carrey) Barish's day doesn't get off to a good start when he discovers that someone has put a big dent in the side of his car – a careless neighbour parking a car alongside Joel's probably. Waiting at the station to catch his train to work, Joel hears platform announcements about a train going to Montauk, Long Island, from the opposite platform. He is seized by an irrational but irresistible urge to go there, and so races across the footbridge to jump on the train before it leaves. While he is walking on the beach, he finds himself attracted to a girl with brightly-dyed hair. It seems it might be mutual, but Joel is acutely shy and cannot bring himself to initiate a conversation. They meet again on the station and sit near each other on the return train. Soon the girl, Clementine Kruczynski (Kate Winslet), starts talking to Joel. She is extremely extrovert and somewhat weird. Joel is flattered by the attention but is also somewhat discomfited. They have a feeling they recognise each other. Despite being polar opposites in terms of character, somehow they click. Joel goes back to Clementine's apartment for a drink and leaves with her telephone number. Their first date is the following evening – they go to the frozen Charles River and lie talking on the ice. The following morning Joel drives Clementine back to her apartment, but she wants to go to his place to sleep so goes in to get her things.

Clementine also picks up her post which includes a letter from a former employee of Lacuna Inc. – a company which provides a memory wiping service. The envelope includes a cassette tape which Clementine plays in the car. It's a recording of her interview with the man who runs the company, Dr. Howard Mierzwiak

(Tom Wilkinson), in which she tells how she wants all memories of her boyfriend Joel Barrish to be erased. Their feeling of having recognised each other was correct – they had shared their lives for well over a year but neither of them has any memory of it.

It transpires that Joel had met Clementine on a beach at a friend's barbecue around eighteen months previously. He was living with someone else at the time, but Clem had the kind of qualities a quiet man such as Joel could not ignore – always speaking her mind, breaking the rules, dyeing her hair to match her mood. They began a relationship. Some time later, however, the inevitable personality clashes drove a wedge between them. After a bitter row, Clem left. Joel decided that he wanted to try to work things out, but was confused when a visit to the bookshop where she works drew a blank – it was as if she didn't even recognise him. Worse still, she greeted some other man as if he was her lover.

Joel went to their mutual friends for an explanation. Eventually they told Joel that Clem had him erased from her memory by Lacuna Inc. (www.lacunainc.com). Furious, Joel decided to have the procedure himself so that he could forget all about Clementine. As the procedure took place, the memories were gradually wiped, starting with the newest and working back to the oldest, deepest memories. This film is Joel's emotional journey through his own brain as he discovers how he really feels about the woman he has paid to forget.[1]

Background

American screenwriter Charlie Kaufman and French director Michel Gondry first collaborated on *Human Nature* (2001). Kaufman is well known for producing unusual scripts that push the boundaries of reality and truth, most notably in *Being John Malkovich* (1999) and *Adaptation* (2002), both in collaboration with director Spike Jonze. Kaufman says,

> 'I think what I like is a director who is interested in the characters of the story, above all else. And understands the intentions of the script and is not only willing, but happy to work with me in collaboration on the project. Those are the things I want in a director, and I feel I have those in Michel and Spike. They both have those qualities.'[2]

Like Jonze, Michel Gondry is a pioneering director of pop music promotional videos. He is likely to be the source of the idea that became 'Bullet Time' – a camera technique used to great effect in the *Matrix* trilogy to capture frozen moments in three dimensions.

Questions for Discussion

1. What triggers the end of Joel's relationship with Clementine?
2. Why does Joel go to Montauk beach on Valentine's Day?
3. 'Why do I fall in love with every woman I see who shows me the least bit of attention?' (Joel, writing in his journal).
   What do you think Joel is looking for in a relationship?
4. 'I apply my personality in a paste' (Clementine, talking about her hair dye).

Eternal Sunshine of the Spotless Mind – *Study Guide* 85

How would you describe Clementine? What does she struggle with? What significance do you think there is in the names of the hair dyes she uses (e.g. Blue Ruin, Rebel Red)?

5. Why do you think Clementine attracts the kind of men who believe she can 'save' them?

6. Why is Clementine so distraught and confused after she has had the memory erasing procedure? Why do you think she gets so upset with Patrick (Elijah Wood)?

7. 'I could die right now, Clem. I'm just happy. I've never felt that before' (Joel).

    Why does Joel want to stop the procedure of memory erasure once it has begun?

8. 'I'm always anxious I'm not living my life to the full' (Clementine).

    What does 'living life to the full' mean to Clementine? What does it mean to you? How do these answers compare with what Jesus is talking about in John 10:10 where he says, 'My purpose is to give life in all its fullness'?

9. 'Blessed are the forgetful for they get the better even of their blunders'[3] (Mary Svevo (Kirsten Dunst), quoting Nietzsche to Dr. Howard Mierzwiak).

    Do these characters do better for erasing one another from their memories?

10. 'How happy is the blameless vestal's lot! The world forgetting, by the world forgot. Eternal sunshine of the spotless mind!'[4] (Mary, quoting Alexander Pope to Howard).

'It's amazing, what Howard does – start over again ... Howard makes it all go away' (Mary to Stan (Mark Ruffalo)).

Why does Mary think that Howard has something great to offer the world with his procedure of memory erasure? What are the similarities and differences between this and God's offer to forgive us and remember our sins no more (Jeremiah 31:34)?

11. Why had Mary gone through with the procedure herself? Had it worked?

12. 'She was not happy and wanted to move on. We provide that possibility' (Howard).

    How do people move on from difficult times in their lives? What difference does being a Christian make? How should a Christian think about such times (see, for example, Psalm 51; 2 Corinthians 4:7–18; Colossians 3:1–15)?

13. Clementine [as the last, but happiest, memory is erased]: 'This is it, Joel. It's gonna be gone soon. What do we do?'
    Joel: 'Enjoy it.'

    Why is it important to remember 'the good times' when relationships become difficult?

14. What – and how – does Joel learn in this movie? How does he discover that he still loves Clementine? Do you think that he does really love her, or are his feelings only related to romantic memories of the early part of their relationship?

15. 'What a loss to spend that much time on someone and to find that she's a stranger' (Joel's recording of why he wants to erase Clementine from his memory).

Why do you think Joel goes after Clem once the truth has been revealed? Why is he willing to accept the consequences of starting again? How do you think the story would develop from this point?

16. 'It was important for me to put something out in the world that seems true. There's a lot of lying going on which has been very detrimental to my existence. Watching movies growing up, I thought, "This is what I'm looking for in a relationship," and because of those movies I constantly found less. This one comes with warts and all, and I refuse to put a moral on it' (Charlie Kaufman).[5]

    Where do you see truth in this movie? Where do you see untruth?

17. What would you most like to forget? Is it really possible to forgive and forget? Which is better, to forgive or to forget? How does/should it change your life to both forgive and be forgiven (see Matthew 18:21–35)?

18. 'It's sometimes not worth going through it. There are too many reasons not to be together ... I couldn't have played this without feeling that loss. Without feeling that someone has erased you ... No, I wouldn't erase any memories. My memories made me what I am' (Jim Carrey).[6]

    To what extent do our memories define who we are today? If you could erase a person from your memory, who would it be? How would it change you?

19. If you could start a relationship again from scratch, do you think you would still come to the same conclusions about one another? How could you

avoid making the same mistakes? Given that you can't start from scratch, how should you behave in your relationships from this point on (see Galatians 5:13–6:10; Ephesians 4:1–16; Philippians 2:1–13)?

Notes

[1] For help in tying together the actual sequence of events, see pedia.newsfilter.co.uk/wikipedia/e/et/eternal_sunshine_of_the_spotless_mind.html

[2] 'Charlie Kaufman: Writer, executive producer *Eternal Sunshine of the Spotless Mind*' on usatoday.com, 8 April 2004 – cgi1.usatoday.com/mchat/20040408003/tscript.htm

[3] Friedrich Nietzsche, *Beyond Good and Evil: Prelude to a Philosophy of the Future*, 217. Ian Johnston translates the phrase as 'Blessed are the forgetful, for they are done with their stupidities as well' – www.mala.bc.ca/~johnstoi/Nietzsche/beyondgoodandevil7.htm

[4] Alexander Pope, 'Eloisa to Abelard' – eir.library.utoronto.ca/rpo/display/poem1630.html

[5] Charlie Kaufmann, 'Love Story', *Empire*, May 2004, p. 99

[6] Jim Carrey, 'Fears of a Clown', *Empire*, May 2004, p. 94

It is a truth universally acknowledged, that a single man in possession of a good fortune, must be in want of a wife.

Jane Austen

8. *The History of Love* – Study Guide

Tony Watkins

Book Title: *The History of Love*
Author: Nicole Krauss
Publisher: Viking
Publication Date: 26 May 2005

Key Themes

Love, loss, history, relationships, families, friendship, truth, honesty, books

Summary

Leo Gursky has lived alone since he arrived in Manhattan from Poland after the war. The love of his life moved there just before the war, but when the Nazis came to their home town, the Jewish Leo hid in the forest and managed to evade them for the next three and a half years. But from the lack of letters, his sweetheart concluded that Leo was dead. By the time he reached her, she had married someone else – she had been pregnant when she left and the little boy needed a father. Leo could never bring himself to love anyone else and he watched his son grow up from a distance, following his eventual career as a famous writer.

Elsewhere in New York lives a young girl Alma, who is named after every girl in a book called *The History of Love*. Alma's father, now dead, had given the book to her mother years ago. Alma wants to find someone for her mother to love again, so when a letter from a man arrives asking Alma's mother to translate *The History of Love* for him, she decides this is a good opportunity to try to steer the course of events.

But she becomes intrigued by the Alma in the book. A Polish man living in Chile had written *The History of Love* and had given all the characters Spanish names except the girls, all of whom are called Alma. Young Alma concludes that the author had been in love with her, and since the book tells about Alma Mereminski coming to New York before the war, she decides to track her down. But the trail takes her in surprising directions.

Background

The History of Love is Nicole Krauss's second novel and continues with the theme of nostalgia and loss from her first, *Man Walks Into a Room.* When she was at school, her teacher said that Gabriel Garcia Marquez's *One Hundred Years of Solitude* is all about nostalgia. Krauss says that she suddenly realised that this was, 'A word for the thing I feel.' But she couldn't see how a teenager could be nostalgic – until she realised that the experience of loss is part of Jewish culture since the Second World War. *The History of Love* arises partly from her family's experience – her great-grandparents and a number of great uncles and aunts died in the Holocaust, and others in the family moved to America. Krauss says, 'I think it has something to do with – or everything to do with – the fact that my grandparents came from these places that we could never go back to, because they'd been lost.'[1] She also comments in the same interview that, 'When the word nostalgia was coined in the 18th century, it was used to describe a pathology – not so much a sense of lost time, but a severe homesickness.'

The History of Love – which is dedicated to her grandparents and to her husband, the author Jonathan Safran Foer – is also about books and the effect they can have on readers. The book at the centre of this novel profoundly influences the lives of most of the characters in some way or other, and it is the threads of its influence – and what lies behind its conception – which Krauss ties together in this multi-layered narrative. She says:

> 'When I started, I'd decided to write a book with no plot. Devising plots didn't seem like my strength, which didn't bother me too much, since the books I love generally don't depend on them. For a long time all I had was Leo's voice. Then Alma's. I had these little bits of *The History of Love* which I didn't know yet were going to become a book within a book – they were just vignettes. I had no idea how all of these elements could possibly fit together. But I also had a sense that they belonged together. It was a struggle to figure out how to connect them to form a constellation. I was always on the edge of failure. I worked myself into so many corners, and dug myself so many holes, and had to try to find intricate, intelligent ways out of them. It was kind of like a game of Twister: how

do I get my toe on the red circle all the way over there?'[2]

The History of Love is to be filmed by Alfonso Cuarón, who previously directed *Harry Potter and the Prisoner of Azkaban* (2004) and is also making a film of Yann Martel's *Life of Pi*.

Questions for Discussion

1. What did you particularly enjoy about *The History of Love?* Was there anything about it you didn't enjoy?
2. What emotional impact did the book have on you? How did the pervading sense of loss within the stories affect you?
3. How does the Second World War continue to exert an influence over the lives of the characters in this novel? Was your understanding of the Holocaust changed in any way as a result of reading *The History of Love?* How?
4. 'And so he did the hardest thing he'd ever done in his life: he picked up his hat and walked away. And if the man who once upon a time had been a boy who promised he'd never fall in love with another girl as long as he lived kept his promise, it wasn't because he was stubborn or even loyal. He couldn't help it' (p. 13). Describe the character of Leo Gursky. What is his outlook on life? Why does he keep going?
5. Of all his son's stories, Leo's favourite is *Glass Houses* about an angel who lives in New York and

becomes angry with God for all the suffering he sees in the world. Why do you think this is Leo's favourite? What do you think Leo's view of God is? What is the book's overall perspective on God? How would you want to respond to this with a biblical view of God?

6. What do you think is going on with Leo and Bruno? Why do you think Leo says, 'He's the friend I didn't have' and 'the greatest character I ever wrote' (p. 249)?

7. How would you describe Alma? Why do you think she is so obsessed with survival skills?

8. How have Alma's family dealt with the death of her father? What do you think of Alma's attempts to find someone for her mother to love?

9. Why does Alma become so preoccupied with finding Alma Mereminski? What is she really looking for?

10. Why does Bird behave in the ways he does, even believing himself to be a Messiah? How do those around him feel about this? Why?

11. Could you understand why Zvi Litvinoff copied out *The History of Love?* How would things have been different for everybody if he hadn't done so?

12. *The History of Love* is 'a book about the way in which books can change people's lives.'[3] In what ways did books change the lives of the characters in the story? Did this book change you in any way? What other books have changed your life? How should the book of God's words affect

you (see Psalm 19:7–14; 119:97–104; 2 Timothy 3:14–17)? How could you allow it to impact on you more?

13. What things do the characters in this novel regret? How do they deal with it? How could an understanding of Psalms 73 and 103 have helped them?

14. What kinds of love, if any, do the characters in *The History of Love* experience in their day to day lives? How do they express their longing for love? Why do human beings have this longing (see Genesis 1:26–28; 2:18–24; 1 John 4:7–8)?

15. 'Later – when things happened that they could never have imagined – she wrote him a letter that said: *When will you learn that there isn't a word for everything?'* (p. 11). Why does Leo decide to call his book *Words for Everything?* In what ways are words central to this story?

16. 'So many words get lost. They leave the mouth and lose their courage, wandering aimlessly until they are swept into the gutter like dead leaves.... There was a time when it wasn't uncommon to use a piece of string to guide words that otherwise might falter on the way to their destinations.... Sometimes no length of string is long enough to say the thing that needs to be said. In such cases all the string can do, in whatever its form, is conduct a person's silence' (p. 111). What does *The History of Love* say about communication between people? What does the Bible say about how we should communicate (see, for example, Proverbs 10:18–21; 12:6, 18–19, 25; 13:3; 15:1–4; 16:23–24; James 3:1–12)?

Notes

[1] Nicole Krauss, *The Observer*, 15 May 2005 – books.guardian.co.uk/departments/generalfiction/story/0,6000,1484082,00.html
[2] Penguin.co.uk – www.penguin.co.uk/nf/Author/AuthorPage/0,,0_1000066500,00.html?sym=QUE
[3] Nicole Krauss, *The Observer*, 15 May 2005

I fell in love with football as I would
later fall in love with women:
suddenly, uncritically, giving no
thought to the pain it would bring.

Nick Hornby, *Fever Pitch*

9. Out of Control – the Philosophy of Arthur Schopenhauer

Peter S. Williams

> 'The Zeitgeist of every age is like a sharp east wind which blows through everything. You can find traces of it in all that is done, thought and written, in music and painting, in the flourishing of this or that art: it leaves its mark on everything and everyone.' (Arthur Schopenhauer)

Arthur Schopenhauer (1788–1860) was born in Stutthof (now Sztutowo, Poland) to a middle class family. When the city fell to Prussia in 1793, Schopenhauer's family fled to Hamburg. His father died, possibly by suicide, in 1807, and his mother – with whom he did not have a good relationship – moved to Weimar. Schopenhauer obtained a PhD from the University of Jena and became a philosophy lecturer at the University of Berlin in 1820, but from 1814–1818 Schopenhauer lived in Dresden working on his most famous book, *The World as Will and Representation*.

From Kant to Will

Taking his inspiration from Immanuel Kant (1724–1804), Schopenhauer divided reality into the way things appear to us (which Kant called *phenomenon*) and the way things are in themselves (which Kant called *noumenon* or *Ding an Sich*, the 'Thing in Itself'). Schopenhauer observed that humans know everything in the world (even their own bodies) from the outside *as objects*, but that they know themselves from the inside *as subjects who will*. Schopenhauer drew an analogy between the outside-in knowledge and Kant's *phenomenon*, and so used the word *representations* for the way things appear to us. He also drew an analogy between the inside-out knowledge and Kant's *noumenon*, and identified the way things are in themselves with something he called *Will*. However, Schopenhauer's *Will* is only an analogy; it does not imply that reality in and of itself is personal.

In *The Discarded Image*, C. S. Lewis observes that the basic idea of modern science is that of natural 'laws', and of events that happen in 'obedience' to them, whereas in medieval science, 'the fundamental concept was that of certain sympathies, antipathies, and strivings inherent in matter itself.'[1] For the modern scientist, every falling body illustrates the 'law' of gravity. For the medieval scientist ('natural philosopher'), every falling body illustrated the 'kindly encycling' of terrestrial bodies to their 'kindly stede' the Earth. For example, Francis Bacon described magnetism by saying that iron, 'in particular sympathy moveth to the lodestone'.[2] However, says Lewis, medieval thinkers did not (in general) believe inanimate objects were *really* sentient or purposive. Bacon did not think that iron objects were *literally* striving for the loadstone:

'If we could ask the medieval scientist, "Why, then, do you talk as if they did?" he might ... retort with the counter-question, "But do you intend your language about *laws* and *obedience* any more literally than I intend mine about *kindly encycling*? Do you really believe that a falling stone is aware of a directive issued to it by some legislator and feels either a moral or a prudential obligation to conform?" We should then have to admit that both ways of expressing the facts are metaphorical.'[3]

In the same way, Schopenhauer's medieval-sounding talk of reality as *Will* is also metaphorical. *Will* is more literally described as:

> 'a mindless, aimless, non-rational urge at the foundation of all our instinctual drives, and at the foundational being of everything.'[4]

So although Schopenhauer begins by interpreting the world using *personal* concepts taken from human experience, his notion of the *Will* actually ends up

> 'demoting humanity from any special status separate from the rest of nature [for] in our bodies, the same "blind" force operates as throughout nature ... Schopenhauer sees the human capacities for perception, rationality, and action as an offshoot of the same wider principle which leads insects to build nests, feathers to grow, and cells to divide.'[5]

As Lewis argued in *The Discarded Image* (and elsewhere at greater length[6]), such a reduction poses problems for belief in rationality:

> 'No Model yet devised has made a satisfactory unity between our actual experience of sensation or thought or emotion and any available account of the corporeal processes which they are held to involve. We experience, say, a chain of reasoning; thoughts, which are "about" or "refer to" something other than themselves, are linked together by the logical relations of grounds and

consequents. Physiology resolves this into a sequence of cerebral events. But physical events, as such, cannot in any intelligible sense be said to be "about" or to "refer to" anything. And they must be linked to one another not as grounds and consequents but as causes and effects – a relation so irrelevant to the logical linkage that it is just as perfectly illustrated by the sequence of a maniac's thoughts as by the sequence of a rational man's.'[7]

Schopenhauer's worldview – despite being framed in the language of individual agency rather than the language of abstract principles – is just as reductionist[8] as that of contemporary materialists who think that only physical matter exists. Schopenhauer's use of the word *Will* gives the impression that his view of reality is directed towards some goal or purpose (teleological), but is this any different to modern day naturalist Richard Dawkins talking about 'selfish genes'? In both cases, the analogy is not meant to imply that inanimate objects are really *trying* to achieve anything. Schopenhauer's *Will*, like Dawkin's *Watchmaker*, is blind.

Kant thought of the *noumenon* (the way things are in themselves) as the objective reality which exists outside of our experience of phenomena – and which is the cause of it. Schopenhauer thought of *Will* and phenomenal experience as *one and the same reality* regarded from different perspectives. They are two sides of the same coin (albeit a coin in which the *Will* side ultimately calls the shots).

Lacking Kant's belief in God, Schopenhauer's worldview gives pride of place to an impersonal, mindless, aimless, amoral and non-rational *Will* to which everything can ultimately be reduced. For example, for Schopenhauer the action of the body is *nothing but* the primal act of *Will* objectified – that is to say, translated into perception. When our bodies do something, we are able to perceive it – and what we are perceiving is the consequence of the fundamental act of *Will*:

> 'Schopenhauer takes a philosophical leap, and uses the double knowledge [from inside and from outside] of his own body as the key to the inner being of every other natural phenomenon. He consequently regards every object in the world as being double-aspected, and as having an inside or inner aspect of its own, just as his consciousness is the inner aspect of his body.'[9]

Hence Schopenhauer says that:

> 'Teeth, gullet, and intestinal canal are objectified hunger; the genitals are objectified sexual impulse; grasping hands and nimble feet correspond to the more indirect strivings of the will which they represent.'[10]

However, it is *Will*, and not individual consciousness, that is the ultimate driving force of every reality – *including the individual consciousness*. In other words, it is something at work deep within us – deeper than conscious or even subconscious thought. Schopenhauer's view of the world is:

> 'Frightening and pandemonic: he maintains that the world as it is in itself ... is an endless striving and blind impulse with no end [goal] in view, devoid of knowledge ... the world is conceived of as being utterly meaningless. When anthropomorphically considered, the world is represented as being in a condition of eternal frustration, as it endlessly strives for nothing in particular, and as it goes essentially nowhere. It is a world far beyond any ascriptions of good and evil.'[11]

If *Will* is a blind impulse without any goals in view, how can we trust our own minds (which are supposedly nothing but *Will* viewed from a different perspective) to be reliably aimed at the goal of knowing the truth about reality? Then again, in his 'Essay on Free Will' (1839) Schopenhauer commits himself to determinism, believing that everything which *does* happen *has to* happen, and that every individual act is determined by prior causes. This not only raises problems for belief in rationality, but in moral accountability as well. In Schopenhauer's world there can be *no* moral accountability, because his worldview excludes any distinction between good and evil. Ultimately, all is simply *Will*. Moreover,

> 'to the atheist Schopenhauer, the very idea of an absolute command either trades surreptitiously on the assumption of an absolute being who may issue it, or it is unfounded.'[12]

But are we really prepared to accept that there is no distinction between good and evil? If not, it follows from Schopenhauer's argument that we ought to accept the existence of an absolute being. On the other hand, if we *are* prepared to accept that there is no distinction between good and evil, then we cannot argue that anyone *ought* to believe Schopenhauer's view of the world!

Schopenhauer sought a single, simple theory to explain the ways in which all things behave. In these terms, Schopenhauer is similar to modern-day proponents of scientific reductionism who believe that everything can be understood solely by understanding the component parts. In both cases, the question that must be faced concerns not the *simplicity*, but the all-important *adequacy* of reductionist explanations.

Love is Blind

> 'Only the male intellect, clouded by the sexual impulse, could call the undersized, narrow-shouldered, broad-hipped, and short-legged sex the fair sex; for in this impulse is to be found its whole beauty' (Arthur Schopenhauer, 'On Women').

Schopenhauer's reductionist approach to love has been particularly influential. For the Christian, love is eminently clear sighted, seeing both the good and the bad in the beloved, and forgiving the bad. For Schopenhauer, love is blind, because love is nothing but an expression of the blind, mindless striving of the *Will*:

> 'The will of the species is so much stronger than that of the individual, that the lover shuts his eyes to all the qualities repugnant to him, overlooks everything, misjudges everything, and blinds himself for ever to the object of his passion.'[13]

In Schopenhauer's view, love is really *nothing but* the inherent drive of all living things to reproduce (and this drive is nothing but an objectification of the *Will*). He distinguishes between what is going on at a conscious level when we fall in love (the way things *seem* to us), and the unconscious *Will to Life* that is the *real* explanation for what goes on at a conscious level. One can see a parallel between Schopenhauer's understanding of love and the views of modern-day evolutionary psychologists. As Mark Rowlands comments, Schopenhauer views love as:

> 'simply an expression of the will to life – and, in particular, that part of the will to life concerned with reproduction. That's the whole point of love – it's one of the ways

the will to life has of conning you into reproducing. By making you believe you are in love with someone, and making the other believe they are in love with you, the will to life increases the likelihood of you doing it like you're on the Discovery Channel.'[14]

In other words, Schopenhauer treats love as if it is reducible to sex, and makes no ultimate distinction between sex as expressed in the human animal and in the rest of nature: 'Schopenhauer sees the individual's sexual behaviour as at the beck and call of an impersonal force.'[15] Schopenhauer's philosophy of love finds expression in such self-justifyng contemporary sayings as, 'Love is blind' and 'The heart wants what the heart wants' which remove all sexually motivated behaviour from the realm of morality.

Moreover, Schopenhauer argues that there is a distinction between what is good for reproduction and what is good for the individual. The *Will to Life* is concerned with producing healthy children. The *Will to Life* therefore directs us towards mating with the people most suited to producing the 'fittest' children. This idea has unfortunate consequences, in that the sort of person 'chosen' for you by the *Will to Life* on the basis of their child-producing potential might not be the right sort of person for you personally. Indeed, the production of healthy children may require that you mate with someone who is temperamentally unsuited to you. Hence, Schopenhauer coins the idea that opposites attract:

'Everyone endeavours to eliminate through the other individual his own weaknesses, defects, and deviations from the type, lest they be perpetuated or even grow into complete abnormalities in the child which will be produced.'[16]

Schopenhauer's view of love is quintessentially modern. For him, love is nothing but the amoral expression of a sexual urge aimed at nothing but the survival of the fittest. While not wishing to deny the existence of biological and sub-conscious bases of physical attraction and erotic love, we may well question whether even erotic love is *nothing but* its biological and sub-conscious components, whether it is aimed at *nothing but* the production of healthy children, and whether it really is doomed to be 'blind'. Are we really to accept that infidelity and adultery cannot be morally censured because, 'the heart wants what the heart wants'? Surely, the *Will to Life* is not so strong that it cannot be resisted – many people (e.g. nuns and monks) choose to live life as virgins! Schopenhauer's reductive view of love is at odds with a theistic worldview that sees love as an essential part of the ultimate reality: God.

Schopenhauer's Fourfold Root

Inspired by Aristotle's division of explanation into four categories (material, formal, efficient and teleological), Schopenhauer defined four kinds of objects which can be explained: material things (e.g. a cup); abstract concepts (e.g. 'refreshment'); mathematical and geometrical constructions (e.g. one teaspoon of sugar plus one teaspoon of sugar equalling two teaspoons of sugar); and psychologically motivating forces (my wanting a refreshing cup of tea with two sugars in it).

Schopenhauer linked four kinds of explanatory reasoning to these four kinds of objects in a one-to-one correspondence. He associated material things with reasoning in terms of cause and effect; abstract concepts with reasoning in terms of logic; mathematical and geometrical constructs with reasoning in reference to numbers and spaces; and motivating forces with reasoning in terms of intentions. One of Schopenhauer's most significant claims was that the four kinds of explanatory reasoning only run in parallel with each other and cannot be intermixed:

> 'If we begin by choosing a certain style of explanation, then we immediately choose the kinds of objects to which we can refer. Conversely, if we begin by choosing a certain kind of object to explain, then we thereby choose a style of reasoning associated with that kind of object.'[17]

For example, if we choose to explain a material thing, Schopenhauer would say that we *must* explain it only in terms of cause and effect reasoning. (This assertion may be seen as a foreshadowing of the principle of 'methodological naturalism' within the natural sciences – i.e. science proceeds on the basis of only trying to find natural, rather than supernatural, explanations for things.[18]) However, suppose the material object under consideration is, in fact, a product of design (e.g. a statue, a machine, a book, a cup of tea, etc.). Are we really to avoid any reference to intention as an explanation *on principle*? When it comes to explaining the existence of a cup of tea, cause and effect certainly plays a role (for example, boiling water is an effect of electrical energy being turned into kinetic energy by a kettle), but there is also an element of intentional design. Every time a forensic scientist examines a dead body and pronounces that a murder has happened, Schopenhauer's explanatory rule is broken. So which should we discard – Schopenhauer's rule or forensic science?

Salvation

According to Schopenhauer, because all reality is an expression of the blind striving of *Will*, phenomenal existence – our experience of life – is by its very nature filled with suffering. Schopenhauer offers a glimmer of hope in the face of this suffering, in that it can be left behind to the extent that we can forget our phenomenal existence. This can be done, says Schopenhauer, through the appreciation of art (where your focus is on the art and not on yourself, so that you 'might lose contact with the turbulent stream of detailed existence around us'[19]), acts of charity (where your focus is on others and not on yourself), and certain religious disciplines (where your focus is not on yourself). In sum, Schopenhauer argues that the only way to avoid suffering is to avoid desiring. But Alex Scott complains that:

> 'A weakness of Schopenhauer's philosophy is its negativity. Ethical conduct is described as negative, and as requiring a denial of the will-to-live. Ethical concern for others is described as being necessarily contradictory to self-interest. Schopenhauer argues that in order to redeem ourselves we must suspend or deny our own willingness to determine our own actions. This viewpoint is a form of self-contradiction which fails to recognize that rational self-concern may be compatible with moral concern for others.'[20]

It has been observed that, 'In solving/alleviating the fundamental problems of life, Schopenhauer was rare among philosophers in considering philosophy and logic less important ... than art, certain types of charitable practice ("loving kindness", in his terms), and certain forms of religious discipline.'[21] However, although placed within a very different metaphysical context, Christian philosophers would agree that participating in divine love, religious devotion and worship *is* more important (if not more fundamental) than philosophy and logic when it comes to solving or alleviating the fundamental problems of life.

For Schopenhauer, salvation has nothing to do with a change of character (what Christians call 'sanctification') and everything to do with losing one's individual character. Indeed, Schopenhauer thought that one's character cannot change. This is a world away from the Christian belief that the sinful part of any human character can ultimately be rooted out, and a person set free to be who they are meant to be, by the loving power of Christ.

Conclusion

Christopher Janaway acknowledges that:

> 'As an exercise in metaphysics, Schopenhauer's doctrine of the will as thing in itself is so obviously flawed that some people have doubted whether he really meant it ... it is perhaps not surprising that his metaphysics has had few followers.'[22]

For example, Janaway argues that Schopenhauer has trouble explaining the knowability of the *Will*:

> 'Even the act of will which we know "immediately" is an event in time, and is therefore part of our representation, rather than the thing in itself ... If knowledge of our acts of will is the nearest we get to the thing in itself, and if

even here we do not know it directly, what grounds do we really have for claiming to know what it is?'[23]

Nevertheless, a number of Schopenhauer's ideas (e.g. 'love is blind', 'opposites attract'), his atheism, and the pessimistic *mood* of his philosophy, have been influential:

> 'Though Schopenhauer's metaphysics is not credible as a system, his questions about the self and the unconscious, action, striving, suffering, renunciation, aesthetic elevation, and the value of existence – the troubling or consoling thoughts that have excited so many influential thinkers – remain alive and challenging.'[24]

Schopenhauer influenced a number of philosophers such as Wittgenstein and Nietzche, whose concept of the *Will to Power* was based on Schopenhauer's *Will to Life*. Schopenhauer's concept of the *Will* contains the germ of what in Freud would become the concept of the unconscious and the id. However, his main influence has been felt though the arts: 'In the late nineteenth and early twentieth centuries ... his books were widely read ... and were seized upon with enthusiasm by intellectuals and artists.'[25] Musicians who fell under Schopenhauer's spell include Richard Wagner, Gustav Mahler and Richard Strauss. Schopenhauer's influence has been particularly strong among literary writers, including Charles Baudelaire, Joseph Conrad, Thomas Hardy, Edgar Allan Poe, Marcel Proust, W. B. Yeats and Emile Zola.

Schopenhauer was prone to depression, and wrote, 'I always have an anxious concern that causes me to see and look for dangers where none exist.'[26] One has to wonder whether there isn't at least an indirect relationship between Schopenhauer's personal depression and his philosophical pessimism. Indeed, one might wonder whether they fed off each other.

Notes

[1] C. S. Lewis, *The Discarded Image*, (Cambridge University Press, 1994), p. 92
[2] Francis Bacon, quoted by C. S. Lewis, *The Discarded Image*, p. 93
[3] C. S. Lewis, *The Discarded Image*, p. 93–94
[4] Robert Wicks, 'Arthur Schopenhauer' in the *Stanford Encyclopedia of Philosophy* – plato.stanford.edu/entries/schopenhauer/
[5] Christopher Janaway, *Schopenhauer: A Very Short Introduction*, (Oxford, 2002), p. 46
[6] cf. C. S. Lewis, *Miracles*, second edition, (Fount, 2002)
[7] C. S. Lewis, *The Discarded Image*, p. 165–166
[8] Reductionism is the belief that everything can be understood solely by understanding its component parts. For example, a reductionist view of a human being is that it is *nothing but* a machine for replicating DNA.
[9] Robert Wicks, 'Arthur Schopenhauer'
[10] Arthur Schopenhauer, *The World as Will and Representation*, vol. 1, (Dover, 1969), p. 108
[11] Robert Wicks, 'Arthur Schopenhauer'
[12] Christopher Janaway, *Schopenhauer: A Very Short Introduction*, (Oxford, 2002), p. 89
[13] Schopenhauer, quoted by Mark Rowlands, *Everything I Know I Learned From TV: Philosophy For The Unrepentent Couch Potato*, (Ebury Press, 2005), p. 156
[14] Mark Rowlands, *Everything I Know I Learned From TV*, p. 153
[15] Christopher Janaway, *Schopenhauer: A Very Short Introduction*, p. 61
[16] Schopenhauer, quoted by Mark Rowlands, *Everything I Know I Learned From TV*, p. 156

[17] Robert Wicks, 'Arthur Schopenhauer'
[18] cf. Alvin Plantinga, 'Methodological Naturalism? Part 1' – www.arn.org/docs/odesign/od181/methnat181.htm and 'Methodological Naturalism? Part 2' – www.arn.org/docs/odesign/od182/methnat182.htm
[19] Henry Alphern, *An Outline History of Philosophy*, quoted on www.blupete.com/Literature/Biographies/Philosophy/Schopenhauer.htm
[20] Alex Scott, 'Schopenhauer's *The World as Will and Idea*' – www.angelfire.com/md2/timewarp/schopenhauer.html
[21] 'Arthur Schopenhauer' in Wikipedia – www.wikipedia.org/wiki/Arthur_Schopenhauer
[22] Christopher Janaway, *Schopenhauer: A Very Short Introduction*, p. 40
[23] Christopher Janaway, *Schopenhauer: A Very Short Introduction*, p. 40
[24] Christopher Janaway, *Schopenhauer: A Very Short Introduction*, p. 127
[25] Christopher Janaway, *Schopenhauer: A Very Short Introduction*, p. 120
[26] Schopenhauer, quoted by Christopher Janaway, *Schopenhauer: A Very Short Introduction*, p. 3

Background to the Featured Quotes

'We are all searching for someone ...'
(p. xv)

'We are all searching for someone. That special person who will provide us what's missing in our lives. Someone who can offer companionship or assistance or security. And sometimes if we search very hard, we can find someone who provides us with all three. Yes, we are all searching for someone. And if we can't find them, we can only pray they find us.'

Mary Alice Young

Source

Desperate Housewives (ABC), series 1, episode 11 – 'Move on'

Background

Desperate Housewives is a US comedy/drama TV series broadcast on Channel 4 in the UK. Hailed as 'the new

Sex and the City', it has been a huge success on both sides of the Atlantic. The first episode, shown in the UK on 5 January 2005, had 5 million viewers, beating the rating figures for the premieres of both *Friends* and *Sex and the City*.

The series centres on a group of women who live in Wisteria Lane, in American suburbia. Our narrator is Mary Alice (Brenda Strong), who, at the beginning of the first episode, talks us through her own suicide. She introduces us to all the mourners at her funeral, and her female friends. The women are all housewives, and they are all desperate in their different ways. Susan (Teri Hatcher) is a divorcee who wants to be loved. Her relationship with new neighbour Mike (James Denton) is developing well. Lynette (Felicity Huffman) left her high-flying career to look after her four unmanagable boys, and is both surprised and frustrated by the demands of this new role. Gabrielle (Eva Longoria) is a former model who has married a fantastically rich man, but she isn't loved and seeks refuge in the arms of her 17-year-old gardener. When husband Carlos gets in trouble with the law, Gabrielle's materialistic outlook is tested. Bree (Marcia Cross) is a control-freak who presents herself as a perfect wife and mother, desperately trying to keep up the façade of happy family life, despite her husband Rex (Steven Culp) asking for a divorce. The series is an ironic look at the American ideal of the suburban family with a stay-at-home Mom keeping the family together.

This quote is Mary Alice's voice-over at the end of episode 11. Bree is considering the possibility of dating someone else now she has discovered Rex's adultery; Felicity is desperate for a nanny to help with her wild children; and Susan has decided she really does love Mike.

'People ... seem to know ...' (p. 13)

> 'People ... seem to know everything about sex but very little about love.'
>
> Rowan Pelling

Source

Interviewed in *Third Way* magazine, March 2004

Background

Rowan Pelling is the former editor of *The Erotic Review*, which she describes as being 'in style ... a sort of hybrid between (if you can imagine such a thing) the *Spectator*, *Private Eye*, *the New Yorker*, I suppose with a splash of *Forum* or something thrown in.'

Pelling was answering a question about whether there are good arguments against promiscuity (she thinks that there are), and expressing the view that she wishes people would talk more about love.

'There's two things I learned ...' (p. 31)

> 'There's two things I learned in life, kid: you find someone to love and live everyday as if it were your last.'
>
> Joe in the film *Alfie*

Source

Alfie (Paramount Pictures, 2004, certificate 15)

Background

Alfie is a remake of the 1966 Michael Caine classic of the same name. The 2004 version moves the action from sixties London to current day New York, and stars Jude Law in the title role of a womanising young man with an aversion to commitment. By the end of the film, Alfie is doubting the merits of his philosophy on life.

Joe (Dick Latessa) is an older man who gets talking to Alfie in the men's room at a doctor's surgery. He tells Alfie how he always threw himself into his work and put off doing lots of things with his wife, who then died before he had the chance to really enjoy spending time with her.

'It changes your life ...' (p. 45)

'It changes your life when you enter into a marriage and it can change it just as much when you're part of a break-up.'

Jude Law

Source

The Sun, 15 January 2004

Background

Popular British actor Jude Law has starred in a string of Hollywood hit movies, including *Gattaca*, *Cold Mountain* and *Closer*. He split from his wife Sadie Frost in 2003 and has joint custody of their three children.

'[Love] is a word . . .' (p. 61)

> '[Love] is a word. What matters is the connection the word implies.'
> Rama Kandra in the film *Matrix Revolutions*

Source

The Matrix Revolutions (Warner Bros 2003, Certificate 15)

Background

The Matrix Revolutions is the third and final film in the *Matrix* trilogy, written and directed by Larry and Andy Wachowski. The trilogy tells the story of the war between humans and machines. In the films, what we think of as real life turns out to be merely a computer generated virtual world, maintained by the machines to keep humanity enslaved. Neo is rescued from the matrix by some human freedom fighters, who believe he is 'the one' – someone born inside the matrix who would liberate humanity. The films are full of spiritual and philosophical references, and when *The Matrix* came out in 1998, many Christians seized on them as an allegory for the gospel message. Closer viewing of *The Matrix* (and indeed its two sequels), however, reveal that the Judeo-Christian imagery did not necessarily present a Christian worldview. For a more in depth analysis of the *Matrix* films, we recommend *Matrix Revelations: A thinking fan's guide to the Matrix Trilogy* (Damaris Books, 2003).

Rama Kandra is a computer program that Neo (Keanu Reeves) meets while marooned in the Train Station. Neo is shocked to discover that programs are able to feel love, which he states to be a human emotion, eliciting the above response.

'That's the problem . . .' (p. 71)

> 'That's the problem with the institution of marriage – it's based on compromise.'
>
> Miles Massey in the film *Intolerable Cruelty*

Source

Intolerable Cruelty (United International Pictures, 2003, certificate 12A)

Background

Miles Massey (played by George Clooney) begins the film as a successful divorce lawyer, but gradually becomes more jaded and disenchanted with his life. At the same time he falls in love with calculating gold-digging divorcee Marilyn (Catherine Zeta-Jones).

Intolerable Cruelty is the tenth film to be written and directed by Joel and Ethan Coen, and is probably the most accessible and commercial film of their career so far. The film is, at times, cynical and dismissive of marriage, but offers a resolution that undermines what has gone before and presents a more positive view of the possibilities of married life.

'You think you've found the right man . . .' (p. 79)

'You think you've found the right man, but there's so much wrong with him. And then he finds there's so much wrong with you. And then it just all falls apart.'
Bridget in the film *Bridget Jones: The Edge of Reason*

Source

Bridget Jones: The Edge of Reason (United International Pictures, 2004, certificate 15)

Background

Bridget Jones: The Edge of Reason is the long-awaited sequel to the massively popular film *Bridget Jones's Diary* (2001). The second film starts six weeks after the first, and Bridget (Renee Zellweger) has fallen deeply in love with her new boyfriend, the human rights barrister Mark Darcy (Colin Firth). Things are going very well for them, and Bridget and Mark seem to have found their 'happy-ever-after' ending.

However, almost as soon as the opening credits finish, reality begins to creep in. Bridget becomes jealous of Mark's new 22-year-old assistant Rebecca (Jacinda Barrett) and thinks that Mark is having an affair with her. Mark takes Bridget to a Law Society dinner and practically ignores her, showing his more haughty and arrogant side. They have both discovered that their partner is not perfect, and this causes them some relationship problems.

'It is a truth universally acknowledged ...' (p. 89)

'It is a truth universally acknowledged, that a single man in possession of a good fortune, must be in want of a wife.'

Jane Austen

Source

Jane Austen, *Pride and Prejudice* (1813), opening sentence

Background

Pride and Prejudice is Jane Austen's second published novel (though the third to be written – the publisher to whom she sent *Northanger Abbey* failed to publish it for some years). It is one of the most popular English novels ever written. In 2003, *Pride and Prejudice* came second in the BBC's *Big Read* poll of the nation's favourite books, narrowly beaten by Tolkien's *The Lord of the Rings*. In many other surveys, these two books consistently top the list, though *Pride and Prejudice* is as often placed at number one rather than number two.

There have been numerous film and television adaptations, the most well-known of which is Andrew Davies's 1995 adaptation for the BBC starring Colin Firth as Mr. Darcy and Jennifer Ehle as Elizabeth Bennet. The most recent adaptation for cinemas (Universal Pictures, 2005) is directed by Joe Wright with a screenplay by Deborah Moggach, and stars Matthew MacFadyen and Keira Knightley. Gurinder Chadha's *Bride and Prejudice* is *Pride and Prejudice* with a Bollywood feel.

The quotation above continues:

> 'However little known the feelings or views of such a man may be on his first entering a neighbourhood, this truth is so well fixed in the minds of the surrounding families that he is considered as the rightful property of some one or other of their daughters.'

For more information and online texts of the novels, see 'The Replublic of Pemberley' – www.pemberley.com.

'I fell in love with football ...' (p. 99)

'I fell in love with football as I would later fall in love with women: suddenly, uncritically, giving no thought to the pain it would bring.'

Nick Hornby, *Fever Pitch*

Source

Fever Pitch, by Nick Hornby (Penguin, 1992)

Background

Fever Pitch was best-selling novelist Nick Hornby's first book. Closer to an autobiography than a novel, Hornby tells the story of his obsession with Arsenal football club, musing on the nature of the modern male, of obsession and the appeal of Britain's national sport. The book was a publishing sensation, outselling any previous 'football book'. Building on the impact made by Paul Gascoigne's tears in the 1990 World Cup semi-final, *Fever Pitch* has been credited/blamed by many for football's subsequent rebranding for a wealthier fanbase.

Nick Hornby is also the author of the novels *High Fidelity*, *About A Boy*, *How To Be Good* and *A Long Way Down*, as well as two collections of his journalism *31 Songs* and *Polysyllabic Spree*.

For Further Reading

John Armstrong, *Conditions of Love – the philosophy of intimacy* (Allen Lane, 2002)

Kirsten Birkett, *Essence of Family* (Matthias Media, 2004)

Phillip Jensen & Tony Payne, *Pure Sex* (Matthias Media, 2003)

Nigel Pollock, *The Relationships Revolution* (IVP, 1998)

Mike Starkey, *God, Sex and Generation X: A Search for Lost Wonder* (Triangle, 1997)

Other Titles in the Talking About Series

Truth Wars: Talking About Tolerance

Playing God: Talking About Ethics in Medicine and Technology (due for publication Spring 2006)

Spooked: Talking About the Supernatural (due for publication Spring 2006)

Other Titles from Damaris Books

Get More Like Jesus While Watching TV
by Nick Pollard and Steve Couch

If Only
by Nick Pollard

Back In Time: A thinking fan's guide to Doctor Who
by Steve Couch, Tony Watkins and Peter S. Williams
(due for publication Autumn 2005)

Dark Matter: A thinking fan's guide to Philip Pullman
by Tony Watkins

Matrix Revelations: A thinking fan's guide to the Matrix Trilogy
edited by Steve Couch

I Wish I Could Believe In Meaning
by Peter S. Williams

Teenagers: Why Do They Do That?
by Nick Pollard

DAMARIS — "Relating Christian faith and contemporary culture"

Join Damaris and receive

Discounts on other products from Damaris Books and Damaris Publishing.

Access to Web pages containing up-to-date information about popular culture.

To find out about *free membership* of Damaris go to www.damaris.org

DAMARIS
www.damaris.org

DAMARIS
www.DamarisBooks.com

"Relating Christian faith and contemporary culture"

CultureWatch
(free access website)

CultureWatch explores the message behind the media through hundreds of articles and study guides on films, books, music and television. It is written from a distinctively Christian angle, but is appropriate for people of all faiths and people of no faith at all.

CULTUREWATCH
http://www.damaris.org/cw

DAMARIS
"Relating Christian faith and contemporary culture"

Tools for Talks
(subscription website)

A one-stop preparation shop for Christian speakers and Bible teachers, enabling you to teach the message of the Bible in the language of contemporary popular culture.

Hundreds of quotes and illustrations from the latest films, music and TV with new material added weekly

All this, plus the complete text of the IVP New Bible Commentary and the Index for Hodder and Stoughton's Thematic Study Bible.

tools for Talks
www.toolsfortalks.com

DAMARIS
www.DamarisBooks.com

The Quest
(CD ROM)

Your journey into the heart of spirituality.

Take your own route, take your own time, seek your own answers to the big philosophical and religious questions with this self-updating oracle for your PC.

The Quest grows as you search, with free updates automatically downloaded from the web.

THE QUEST
www.questforanswers.com